2200
10.00

Cakes & Cookies

D1285805

Babylon 2099   11-17-09

Publisher & Creative Director: Nick Wells
Senior Project Editor: Cat Emslie
Art Director: Mike Spender
Digital Design & Production: Chris Herbert

This is a **FLAME TREE** Book

FLAME TREE PUBLISHING
Crabtree Hall, Crabtree Lane
Fulham, London SW6 6TY
United Kingdom
www.flametreepublishing.com

Flame Tree is part of The Foundry Creative Media Company Limited

First published 2009

Copyright © 2009 Flame Tree Publishing

09 11 13 12 10
1 3 5 7 9 10 8 6 4 2

ISBN: 978-1-84786-454-3

All rights reserved. No part of this publication may be reproduced, stored in a retrieval system,
or transmitted in any form or by any means, electronic, mechanical, photocopying, recording or otherwise,
without the prior written permission of the publisher.

A copy of the CIP data for this book is available from the British Library.

Printed in China

Port Colborne Public Library
DISCARD

Cakes & Cookies

Quick and Easy, Proven Recipes

**FLAME TREE
PUBLISHING**

Contents

Brownies & Traybakes

Small Cakes & Buns

Everyday Cakes

Cream Cakes & Special Occasions

Cheesecakes & Cake Puddings

Essential Hygiene in the Kitchen

It is well worth remembering that many foods can carry some form of bacteria. In most cases, the worst it will lead to is a bout of food poisoning or gastroenteritis, although for certain groups this can be more serious. The risk can be reduced or eliminated by good food hygiene and proper cooking.

Do not buy food that is past its sell-by date and do not consume any food that is past its use-by date. When buying food, use the eyes and nose. If the food looks tired, limp or a bad colour or it has a rank, acrid or simply bad smell, do not buy or eat it under any circumstances.

Regularly clean, defrost and clear out the refrigerator or freezer – it is worth checking the packaging to see exactly how long each product is safe to freeze.

Dish cloths and tea towels must be washed and changed regularly. Ideally use disposable cloths which should be replaced on a daily basis. More durable cloths should be

left to soak in bleach, then washed in the washing machine on a boil wash.

Always keep your hands, cooking utensils and food preparation surfaces clean and never allow pets to climb on to any work surfaces.

Buying

Avoid bulk buying where possible, especially fresh produce such as meat, poultry, fish, fruit and vegetables unless buying for the freezer. Fresh foods lose their nutritional value rapidly so buying a little at a time minimises loss of nutrients. It also eliminates a packed refrigerator which reduces the effectiveness of the refrigeration process.

When buying frozen foods, ensure that they are not heavily iced on the outside. Place in the freezer as soon as possible after purchase.

Preparation

Make sure that all work surfaces and utensils are clean and dry. Separate chopping boards should be used for raw and cooked meats, fish and vegetables. It is worth washing all fruits and vegetables regardless of whether they are going to be eaten raw or lightly cooked. Do not reheat food more than once.

All poultry must be thoroughly thawed before cooking. Leave the food in the refrigerator until it is completely thawed. Once defrosted, the chicken should be cooked as soon as possible. The only time food can be refrozen is when the food has been thoroughly thawed then cooked. Once the food has cooled then it can be frozen again for one month.

All poultry and game (except for duck) must be cooked thoroughly. When cooked the juices will run clear. Other meats, like minced meat and pork should be cooked right the way through. Fish should turn opaque, be firm in texture and break easily into large flakes.

Storing, Refrigerating and Freezing

Meat, poultry, fish, seafood and dairy products should all be refrigerated. The temperature of the refrigerator should be between 1–5°C/34–41°F while the freezer temperature should not rise above -18°C/-0.4°F. When refrigerating cooked food, allow it to cool down completely before refrigerating. Hot food will raise the temperature of the refrigerator and possibly affect or spoil other food stored in it.

Food within the refrigerator and freezer should always be covered. Raw and cooked food should be stored in separate parts of the refrigerator. Cooked food should be kept on the top shelves of the refrigerator, while raw meat, poultry and fish should be placed on bottom shelves to avoid drips and cross-contamination.

High-Risk Foods

Certain foods may carry risks to people who are considered vulnerable such as the elderly, the ill, pregnant women, babies and those suffering from a recurring illness. It is advisable to avoid those foods which belong to a higher-risk category.

There is a slight chance that some eggs carry the bacteria salmonella. Cook the eggs until both the yolk and the white are firm to eliminate this risk. Sauces including Hollandaise, mayonnaise, mousses, soufflés and meringues all use raw or lightly cooked eggs, as do custard-based dishes, ice creams and sorbets. These are all considered high-risk foods to the vulnerable groups mentioned above. Certain meats and poultry also carry the potential risk of salmonella and so should be cooked thoroughly until the juices run clear and there is no pinkness left. Unpasteurised products such as milk, cheese (especially soft cheese), pâté, meat (both raw and cooked) all have the potential risk of listeria and should be avoided.

When buying seafood, buy from a reputable source. Fish should have bright clear eyes, shiny skin and bright pink or red gills. The fish should feel stiff to the touch, with a slight smell of sea air and iodine. The flesh of fish steaks and fillets should be translucent with no signs of discolouration. Avoid any molluscs that are open or do not close when tapped lightly. Univalves such as cockles or winkles should withdraw into their shells when lightly prodded. Squid and octopus should have firm flesh and a pleasant sea smell.

Care is required when freezing seafood. It is imperative to check whether the fish has been frozen before. If it has been, then it should not be frozen again under any circumstances.

Nutrition
The Role of Essential Nutrients

A healthy and well-balanced diet is the body's primary energy source. In children, it constitutes the building blocks for future health as well as providing lots of energy. In adults, it encourages self-healing and regeneration within the body. A well-balanced diet will provide the body with all the essential nutrients it needs. This can be achieved by eating a variety of foods, demonstrated in the pyramid below:

Fats
milk, yoghurt
and cheese

Proteins
meat, fish, poultry, eggs,
nuts and pulses

Fruits and Vegetables

Starchy Carbohydrates
cereals, potatoes, bread, rice and pasta

Fats

Fats fall into two categories: saturated and unsaturated fats. It is very important that a healthy balance is achieved within the diet. Fats are an essential part of the diet and a source of energy and provide essential fatty acids and fat soluble vitamins. The right balance of fats should boost the body's immunity to infection and keep muscles, nerves and arteries in good condition. Saturated fats are of animal origin and are hard when stored at room temperature. They can be found in dairy produce, meat, eggs, margarines and hard white cooking fat (lard) as well as in manufactured products such as pies, biscuits and cakes. A high intake of saturated fat over many years has been proven to increase heart disease and high blood cholesterol levels and often leads to weight gain. The aim of a healthy diet is to keep the fat content low in the foods that we eat. Lowering the amount of saturated fat that we consume is very important, but this does not mean that it is good to consume lots of other types of fat.

There are two kinds of unsaturated fats: poly-unsaturated fats and monounsaturated fats. Poly-unsaturated fats include the following oils: safflower oil, soybean oil, corn oil and sesame oil. Within the poly-unsaturated group are Omega oils. The Omega-3 oils are of significant interest because they have been found to be particularly beneficial to coronary health and can encourage brain growth and development. Omega-3 oils are derived from oily fish such as salmon, mackerel, herring, pilchards and sardines. It is recommended that we should eat these types of fish at least once a week. However, for those who do not eat fish or who are vegetarians, liver oil supplements are available in most supermarkets and health shops. It is suggested that these supplements should be taken on a daily basis. The most popular oils that are high in monounsaturates are olive oil, sunflower oil and peanut oil. The Mediterranean diet, which is based on a diet high in mono-unsaturated fats, is recommended for heart health. Also, monounsaturated fats are known to help reduce the levels of LDL (the bad) cholestrol.

Proteins

Composed of amino acids (proteins' building bricks), proteins perform a wide variety of essential functions for the body including supplying energy and building and repairing tissues. Good sources of proteins are eggs, milk, yoghurt, cheese, meat, fish, poultry, eggs, nuts and pulses. (See the second level of the pyramid.) Some of these foods, however, contain saturated fats. To strike a nutritional balance eat generous amounts of vegetable protein foods such as soya, beans, lentils, peas and nuts.

Fruits and Vegetables

Not only are fruits and vegetables the most visually appealing foods, but they are extremely good for us, providing essential vitamins and minerals essential for growth, repair and protection in the human body. Fruits and vegetables are low in calories and are responsible for regulating the body's metabolic processes and controlling the composition of its fluids and cells.

Minerals

CALCIUM Important for healthy bones and teeth, nerve transmission, muscle contraction, blood clotting and hormone function. Calcium promotes a healthy heart, improves skin, relieves aching muscles and bones, maintains the correct acid-alkaline balance and reduces menstrual cramps. Good sources are dairy products, small bones of small fish, nuts, pulses, fortified white flours, breads and green leafy vegetables.

CHROMIUM Part of the glucose tolerance factor, chromium balances blood sugar levels, helps to normalise hunger and reduce cravings, improves lifespan, helps protect DNA and is essential for heart function. Good sources are brewer's yeast, wholemeal bread, rye bread, oysters, potatoes, green peppers, butter and parsnips.

IODINE Important for the manufacture of thyroid hormones and for normal development. Good sources of iodine are seafood, seaweed, milk and dairy products.

IRON As a component of haemoglobin, iron carries oxygen around the body. It is vital for normal growth and development. Good sources are liver, corned beef, red meat, fortified breakfast cereals, pulses, green leafy vegetables, egg yolk and cocoa and cocoa products.

MAGNESIUM Important for efficient functioning of metabolic enzymes and development of the skeleton. Magnesium promotes healthy muscles by helping them to relax and is therefore good for PMS. It is also important for heart muscles and the nervous system. Good sources are nuts, green vegetables, meat, cereals, milk and yoghurt.

PHOSPHORUS Forms and maintains bones and teeth, builds muscle tissue, helps maintain the body's pH and aids metabolism and energy production. Phosphorus is present in almost all foods.

POTASSIUM Enables nutrients to move into cells, while waste products move out; promotes healthy nerves and muscles; maintains fluid balance in the body; helps secretion of insulin for blood sugar control to produce constant energy; relaxes muscles; maintains heart functioning and stimulates gut movement to encourage proper elimination. Good sources are fruit, vegetables, milk and bread.

SELENIUM Antioxidant properties help to protect against free radicals and carcinogens. Selenium reduces inflammation, stimulates the immune system to fight infections, promotes a healthy heart and helps vitamin E's action. It is also required for the male reproductive system and is needed for metabolism. Good sources are tuna, liver, kidney, meat, eggs, cereals, nuts and dairy products.

SODIUM Important in helping to control body fluid and balance, preventing dehydration. Sodium is involved in muscle and nerve function and helps move nutrients into cells. All foods are good sources, however processed, pickled and salted foods are richest in sodium.

ZINC Important for metabolism and the healing of wounds. It also aids ability to cope with stress, promotes a healthy nervous system and brain especially in the growing foetus, aids bones and teeth formation and is essential for constant energy. Good sources are liver, meat, pulses, whole-grain cereals, nuts and oysters.

Vitamins

VITAMIN A Important for cell growth and development and for the formation of visual pigments in the eye. Vitamin A comes in two forms: retinol and beta-carotenes. Retinol is found in liver, meat and meat products and whole milk and its products. Beta-carotene is a powerful antioxidant and is found in red and yellow fruits and vegetables such as carrots, mangoes and apricots.

VITAMIN B1 Important in releasing energy from carboydrate-containing foods. Good sources are yeast and yeast products, bread, fortified breakfast cereals and potatoes.

VITAMIN B2 Important for metabolism of proteins, fats and carbohydrates to produce energy. Good sources are meat, yeast extracts, fortified breakfast cereals and milk and its products.

VITAMIN B3 Required for the metabolism of food into energy production. Good sources are milk and milk products, fortified breakfast cereals, pulses, meat, poultry and eggs.

VITAMIN B5 Important for the metabolism of food and energy production. All foods are good sources but especially fortified breakfast cereals, whole-grain bread and dairy products.

VITAMIN B6 Important for metabolism of protein and fat. Vitamin B6 may also be involved with the regulation of sex hormones. Good sources are liver, fish, pork, soya beans and peanuts.

VITAMIN B12 Important for the production of red blood cells and DNA. It is vital for growth and the nervous system. Good sources are meat, fish, eggs, poultry and milk.

BIOTIN Important for metabolism of fatty acids. Good sources of biotin are liver, kidney, eggs and nuts. Micro-organisms also manufacture this vitamin in the gut.

VITAMIN C Important for healing wounds and the formation of collagen which keeps skin and bones strong. It is an important antioxidant. Good sources are fruits, soft summer fruits and vegetables.

VITAMIN D Important for absorption and handling of calcium to help build bone strength. Good sources are oily fish, eggs, whole milk and milk products, margarine and of course sufficient exposure to sunlight, as vitamin D is made in the skin.

VITAMIN E Important as an antioxidant vitamin helping to protect cell membranes from damage. Good sources are vegetable oils, margarines, seeds, nuts and green vegetables.

FOLIC ACID Critical during pregnancy for the development of the brain and nerves. It is always essential for brain and nerve function and is needed for utilising protein and red blood cell formation. Good sources are whole-grain cereals, fortified breakfast cereals, green leafy vegetables, oranges and liver.

VITAMIN K Important for controlling blood clotting. Good sources are cauliflower, Brussels sprouts, lettuce, cabbage, beans, broccoli, peas, asparagus, potatoes, corn oil, tomatoes and milk.

Carbohydrates

Carbohydrates are an energy source and come in two forms: starch and sugar carbohydrates. Starch carbohydrates are also known as complex carbohydrates and they include all cereals, potatoes, breads, rice and pasta. (See the fourth level of the pyramid). Eating whole-grain varieties of these foods also provides fibre. Diets high in fibre are believed to be beneficial in helping to prevent bowel cancer and can also keep cholesterol down. High-fibre diets are also good for those concerned about weight gain. Fibre is bulky so fills the stomach, therefore reducing hunger pangs. Sugar carbohydrates, which are also known as fast-release carbohydrates (because of the quick fix of energy they give to the body), include sugar and sugar-sweetened products such as jams and syrups. Milk provides lactose, which is a milk sugar, and fruits provide fructose, which is a fruit sugar.

Essential Baking Ingredients

The quantities may differ, but basic baking ingredients do not vary greatly. Let us take a closer look at the baking ingredients which are essential.

Fat

Butter and firm block margarine are the fats most commonly used in baking. Others can also be used such as white vegetable fat, lard and oil. Low-fat spreads are not recommended as they break down when cooked at a high temperature and are not recommended for baking. Often it is a matter of personal preference which fat you choose when baking but there are a few guidelines that are important to remember.

Unsalted butter is the fat most commonly used in cake making, especially in rich fruit cakes and the heavier sponge cakes such as Madeira or chocolate torte. Unsalted butter gives a distinctive flavour to the cake. Some people favour margarine which imparts little or no flavour to the cake. As a rule, firm margarine and butter should not be used straight from the refrigerator but allowed to come to room temperature before using. Also, it should be beaten by itself first before creaming or rubbing in. Soft margarine is best suited to one-stage recipes. If oil is used care should be taken – it is a good idea to follow a specific recipe as the proportions of oil to flour and eggs are different.

Fat is an integral ingredient when making pastry, again there are a few specific guidelines to bear in mind.

For shortcrust pastry the best results are achieved by using equal amounts of lard or white vegetable fat with butter or block margarine. The amount of fat used is always half the amount of flour. Other pastries use differing amounts of ingredients. Pâté sucrée (a sweet flan pastry) uses all butter with eggs and a little sugar, while flaky or puff pastry uses a larger proportion of fat to flour and relies on the folding and rolling during making to ensure that the pastry rises and flakes well. When using a recipe, refer to the instructions to obtain the best result.

Flour

We can buy a wide range of flour all designed for specific jobs. Strong flour which is rich in gluten, whether it is white or brown (this includes granary and stoneground) is best kept for bread and Yorkshire pudding. It is also recommended for steamed suet puddings as well as puff pastry. '00' flour is designed for pasta making and there is no substitute for this

it is possible to buy flours that cater for coeliacs which contain no gluten. Buckwheat, soya and chick pea flours are also available.

Eggs

When a recipe states 1 egg, it is generally accepted this refers to a medium egg. Over the past few years the grading of eggs has changed. For years, eggs were sold as small, standard and large, then this method changed and they were graded in numbers with 1 being the largest. The general feeling by the public was that this system was misleading, so now we buy our eggs as small, medium and

flour. Ordinary flour or weak flour is best for cakes, biscuits and sauces which absorb the fat easily and give a soft light texture. This flour comes in plain white or self-raising, as well as wholemeal. Self-raising flour, which has the raising agent already incorporated is best kept for sponge cakes where it is important that an even rise is achieved. Plain flour can be used for all types of baking and sauces. If using plain flour for scones or cakes and puddings, unless other-wise stated in the recipe, use 1 teaspoon of baking powder to 225 g/8 oz of plain flour. With sponge cakes and light fruit cakes, it is best to use self-raising flour as the raising agent has already been added to the flour. This way there is no danger of using too much which can result in a sunken cake with a sour taste. There are other raising agents that are also used. Some cakes use bicarbonate of soda with or without cream of tartar, blended with warm or sour milk. Whisked eggs also act as a raising agent as the air trapped in the egg ensures that the mixture rises. Generally no other raising agent is required.

Flour also comes ready sifted. There is even a special sponge flour designed especially for whisked sponges. Also,

large. Due to the slight risk of salmonella, all eggs are now sold date stamped to ensure that the eggs are used in their prime. This applies even to farm eggs which are no longer allowed to be sold straight from the farm. Look for the lion quality stamp (on 75% of all eggs sold) which guarantees that the eggs come from hens vaccinated against salmonella, have been laid in the UK and are produced to the highest food safety and standards. All of these eggs carry a best before date.

There are many types of eggs sold and it really is a question of personal preference which ones are chosen. All offer the same nutritional benefits. The majority of eggs sold in this country are caged eggs. These are the cheapest eggs and the hens have been fed on a manufactured mixed diet.

Barn eggs are from hens kept in barns who are free to roam within the barn. However, their diet is similar to caged hens and the barns may be overcrowded.

It is commonly thought that free-range eggs are from hens that lead a much more natural life and are fed natural foods. This, however, is not always the case and in some instances they may still live in a crowded environment.

Four-grain eggs are from hens that have been fed on grain and no preventative medicines have been included in their diet. Organic eggs are from hens that live in a flock, whose beaks are not clipped and who are completely free to roam. Obviously, these eggs are much more expensive than the others.

Store eggs in the refrigerator with the round end uppermost (as packed in the egg boxes). Allow to come to room temperature before using. Do remember, raw or

semi-cooked eggs should not be given to babies, toddlers, pregnant women, the elderly and those suffering from a reccurring illness.

Sugar

Sugar not only offers taste to baking but also adds texture and volume to the mixture. It is generally accepted that caster sugar is best for sponge cakes, puddings and meringues. Its fine granules disperse evenly when creaming or whisking.

Granulated sugar is used for more general cooking, such as stewing fruit, whereas demerara sugar with its toffee taste and crunchy texture is good for sticky puddings and cakes such as flapjacks. For rich fruit cakes, Christmas puddings and cakes, use the muscovado sugars which give a rich intense molasses or treacle flavour. Icing sugar is used primarily for icings and can be used in meringues and in fruit sauces when the sugar needs to dissolve quickly. For a different flavour try flavouring your own sugar. Place a vanilla pod in a screw top jar, fill with caster sugar, screw down the lid and leave for 2–3 weeks before using. Top up after use or use thinly pared lemon or orange rind in the same manner.

If trying to reduce sugar intake then use the unrefined varieties, such as golden granulated, golden caster, unrefined demerara and the muscovado sugars. All of these are a little sweeter than their refined counterparts, so less is required. Alternatively, clear honey or fructose (fruit sugar) can reduce sugar intake as they have similar calories to sugar, but are twice as sweet. Also, they have a slow release so their effect lasts longer. Dried fruits can also be included in the diet to top up sugar intake.

Baking Equipment

Nowadays, you can get lost in the cookware sections of some of the larger stores – they really are a cook's paradise with gadgets, cooking tools and state-of-the-art electronic blenders, mixers and liquidisers. A few, well-picked, high-quality utensils and pieces of equipment will be frequently used and will therefore be a much wiser buy than cheaper gadgets.

Cooking equipment not only assists in the kitchen, but can make all the difference between success and failure. Take the humble cake tin, although a very basic piece of cooking equipment, it plays an essential role in baking. Using the incorrect size, for example, a tin that is too large will spread the mixture too thinly and the result will be a flat, limp-looking cake. On the other hand, cramming the mixture into a tin which is too small will result in the mixture rising up and out of the tin.

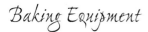

Baking Equipment

To ensure successful baking it is worth investing in a selection of high quality tins, which if looked after properly should last for many years. Follow the manufacturers' instructions when first using and ensure that the tins are thoroughly washed and dried after use and before putting away.

Perhaps the most useful of tins for baking are sandwich cake tins, ideal for classics such as Victoria sponge, genoese and coffee and walnut cake. You will need two tins and they are normally 18 cm/7 inches or 20.5 cm/8 inches in diameter and are about 5–7.5cm/2–3 inches deep and are often non stick.

With deep cake tins, it is personal choice whether you buy round or square tins and they vary in size from 12.5–35.5 cm /5–14 inches with a depth of between 12.5–15 cm/5–6 inches. A deep cake tin, for everyday fruit or Madeira cake is a must, a useful size is 20.5 cm/8 inches.

Loaf tins are used for bread, fruit or tea bread and terrines and normally come in two sizes, 450 g/1 lb and 900 g/2 lb.

Good baking sheets are a must for all cooks. Dishes that are too hot to handle such as apple pies should be placed directly on to the baking tray. Meringues, biscuits and cookies are cooked on the tray. Do not confuse with Swiss roll tins which have sides all around, whereas a sheet only has one raised side.

Square or oblong shallow baking tins are also very useful for making tray bakes, fudge brownies, flapjacks and shortbread.

Then there are patty tins; ideal for making small buns, jam tarts or mince pies; individual Yorkshire pudding tins and muffin tins or flan tins. They are available in a variety of sizes.

There are plenty of other tins to choose from, ranging from themed tins, such as a Christmas trees, numbers from 1–9 as well as tins shaped as petals, ring mould tins, (tins with a hole in the centre) to spring form tins where the sides release after cooking allowing the finished cake to be removed easily.

Three to four different sizes of mixing bowls are also very useful.

Another piece of equipment which is worth having is a wire cooling rack. It is essential when baking to allow biscuits and cakes to cool after being removed from their tins.

A selection of different sized roasting tins are also a worthwhile investment as they can double up as a bain marie, or for cooking larger quantities of cakes such as gingerbread. A few different tins and dishes are required if baking crumbles, soufflés and pies. Ramekin dishes and small pudding basins can be used for a variety of different recipes as can small tartlet tins and dariole moulds.

When purchasing your implements for baking, perhaps the rolling pin is one of the most important. Ideally it should be long and thin, heavy enough to roll the pastry out easily but not too heavy that it is uncomfortable to use. Pastry needs to be rolled out on a flat surface and although a lightly floured flat surface will do, a marble slab will ensure that the pastry is kept cool and ensures that the fats do not melt while being rolled. This helps to keep the pastry light, crisp and flaky rather than heavy and stodgy which happens if the fat melts before being baked.

Other useful basic pastry implements are tools such as a pastry brush (which can be used to wet pastry or brush on a glaze), a pastry wheel for cutting and a sieve to remove impurities and also to sift air into the flour, encouraging the pastry or mixture to be lighter in texture.

Basic mixing cutlery is also essential such as a wooden spoon (for mixing and creaming), a spatula (for transferring the mixture from the mixing bowl to the baking tins and spreading the mixture once it is in the tins) and a palette knife (to ease cakes and breads out of their tins before placing them on the wire racks to cool). Measuring spoons are essential for accurate measuring of both dry and wet ingredients.

Electrical Equipment

Nowadays help from time-saving gadgets and electrical equipment make baking far easier and quicker. Equipment can be used for creaming, mixing, beating, whisking and kneading, grating and chopping. There is a wide choice of machines available from the most basic to the very sophisticated.

Food Processors

First decide what you need your processor to do when choosing a machine. If you are a novice to baking, it may be a waste to start with a machine which offers a wide range of implements and functions. This can be off putting and result in not using the machine to its ultimate.

In general, while styling and product design play a role in the price, the more you pay, the larger the machine will be with a bigger bowl capacity and many more gadgets attached. Nowadays, you can chop, shred, slice, chip, blend, purée, knead, whisk and cream anything. However, just what basic features should you ensure your machine has before buying it?

When buying a food processor look for measurements on the side of the processor bowl and machines with a removable feed tube which allows food or liquid to be added while the motor is still running. Look out for machines that have the facility to increase the capacity of the bowl (ideal when making soup) and have a pulse button for controlled chopping.

For many, storage is an issue so reversible discs and flex storage, or on more advanced models, a blade storage compartment or box, can be advantageous.

It is also worth thinking about machines which offer optional extras which can be bought as your cooking requirements change. Mini-chopping bowls are available for those wanting to chop small quantities of food. If time is an issue, dishwasher-friendly attachments may be vital. Citrus presses, liquidisers and whisks may all be useful attachments for the individual cook.

Blenders

Blenders often come as attachments to food processors and are generally used for liquidising and puréeing foods. There are two main types of blender. The first is known as a goblet blender. The blades of this blender are at the bottom of the goblet with measurements up the sides. The second blender is portable. It is hand-held and should be placed in a bowl to blend.

Food Mixers

These are ideally suited to mixing cakes and kneading dough, either as a table-top mixer or a hand-held mixer. Both are extremely useful and based on the same principle of mixing or whisking in an open bowl to allow more air to get to the mixture and therefore give a lighter texture.

The table-top mixers are freestanding and are capable of dealing with fairly large quantities of mixture. They are robust machines, capable of easily dealing with kneading dough and heavy cake mixing as well as whipping cream, whisking egg whites or making one-stage cakes. These mixers also offer a wide range of attachments ranging from liquidisers, mincers, juicers, can openers and many more and varied attachments.

Hand-held mixers are smaller than freestanding mixers and often come with their own bowl and stand from which they can be lifted off and used as hand-held devices. They have a motorised head with detachable twin whisks. These mixers are particularly versatile as they do not need a specific bowl in which to whisk. Any suitable mixing bowl can be used.

Handling Chocolate: Tips & Techniques

There are a few useful techniques for working with chocolate. None of them are very complicated, and all can be mastered easily with a little practice. These general guidelines apply equally for all types of chocolate.

Melting chocolate

All types of chocolate are sensitive to temperature, so care needs to be taken during the melting process. It is also worth noting that different brands of chocolate have different consistencies when melting and when melted. Experiment with different brands to find one that you prefer.

As a general rule, it is important not to allow any water to come into contact with the chocolate. In fact, a drop or two of water is more dangerous than larger amounts, which may blend in. The melted chocolate will seize and it will be impossible to bring it back to a smooth consistency.

Do not overheat chocolate or melt it by itself in a pan over a direct heat. Always use either a double boiler or a heatproof bowl set over a saucepan of water, but do not allow the bottom of the bowl to come into contact with the water as this would overheat the chocolate. Keep an eye on the chocolate, checking it every couple of minutes and reducing or extinguishing the heat under the saucepan, as necessary. Stir the chocolate once or twice during melting until it is smooth and no lumps remain. Do not cover the bowl once the chocolate has melted or condensation will form, water will drop into it and it will be ruined. If the chocolate turns from a glossy, liquid mass into a dull, coarse, textured mess, you will have to start again.

Microwaving is another way of melting chocolate, but again, caution is required. Follow the oven manufacturer's instructions together with the instructions on the chocolate and proceed with care. Melt the chocolate in bursts of 30–60 seconds, stirring well between bursts until the chocolate is smooth. If possible, stop microwaving before all the chocolate has melted and allow the residual heat in the chocolate to finish the job. The advantage of microwaving is that you do not need to use a saucepan, making the whole job quicker and neater.

Making Chocolate Decorations

CURLS AND CARAQUE Chocolate curls are made using a clean paint scraper. They are usually large, fully formed curls which are useful for decorating gateaux and cakes. Caraque are long thin curls which can be used in the same way, but are less dramatic.

To make either shape, melt the chocolate following your preferred method and then spread it in a thin layer over a cool surface, such as a marble slab, ceramic tile or piece of granite. Leave until just set but not hard.

To make curls, take the clean paint scraper and set it at an angle to the surface of the chocolate, then push, taking a layer off the surface. This will curl until you release the pressure.

To make caraque, use a large sharp knife and hold it at about a 45-degree angle to the chocolate. Hold the handle and the tip and scrape the knife towards you pulling the handle but keeping the tip more or less in the same place. This method makes thinner, tighter, longer curls.

SHAVED CHOCOLATE Using a vegetable peeler, shave a thick block of chocolate to make mini-curls. These are best achieved if the chocolate is a little soft, otherwise it has a tendency to break into little flakes.

CHOCOLATE SHAPES Spread a thin layer of chocolate, as described in the instructions for chocolate curls, and allow to set as before. Use shaped cutters or a sharp knife to cut out shapes. Use to decorate cakes.

CHOCOLATE LEAVES Many types of leaf are suitable, but ensure they are not poisonous before using. Rose leaves are easy to find and make good shapes. Wash and dry the leaves carefully before using. Melt chocolate following the instructions given at the beginning of the section. Using a small paintbrush, paint a thin layer of chocolate on to the back of the leaf. Allow to set before adding another thin layer. When set, carefully peel off the leaf. Chocolate leaves are

CHOCOLATE LACE Make a non stick baking parchment piping bag. Draw an outline of the required shape onto some nonstick baking parchment, a triangle, for example. Pipe chocolate evenly onto the outline, fill in the centre with lacy squiggles and leave until set. Remove the paper to use.

CHOCOLATE SQUIGGLES Use a teaspoon of melted chocolate to drizzle random shapes on to nonstick baking parchment. Leave to set and remove paper to use. Alternatively, pipe a zigzag line about 5 cm/2 inches long on to a piece of nonstick baking parchment. Pipe a straight line slightly longer at either end down the middle of the zigzag.

CHOCOLATE MODELLING PASTE To make chocolate modelling paste (very useful for cake coverings and for making heavier shapes, like ribbons) put 200 g/7 oz plain chocolate in a bowl and add 3 tablespoons of liquid glucose.

also very attractive when made using two different types of chocolate, white and dark chocolate, for example. Paint half the leaf first with one type of chocolate and allow to set before painting the other half with the second chocolate. Leave to set then peel off the leaf as above.

CHOCOLATE BUTTERFLIES Draw a butterfly shape on a piece of nonstick baking parchment. Fold the paper down the middle of the body of the butterfly to make a crease, then open the paper out flat. Pipe chocolate on to the outline of the butterfly, then fill in the wings with loose zigzag lines. Carefully fold the paper so the wings are at right-angles, supporting them from under-neath in the corner of a large tin or with some other support, and leave until set. Peel away the paper to use.

plunge the base of the pan into cold water to stop it from cooking further.

PRALINE To make praline, follow the instructions as for caramel but during the final stage do not plunge the pan into cold water. Add nuts to the caramel mixture, do not stir, but pour immediately on to an oiled baking sheet. Leave to set at room temperature. Once cold, the praline can be chopped or broken into pieces as required. Keep leftover praline in a sealed container. It will keep for several months if stored this way.

CARAMEL-DIPPED NUTS Make the caramel, remove the pan from the heat and plunge into cold water as described earlier. Using two skewers or two forks, dip individual nuts into the hot caramel, lift out carefully, allowing excess to run off, then transfer to a foil-covered tray until set. If the caramel becomes too sticky or starts making a lot of sugar strands, reheat gently until liquid again.

Set the bowl over a pan of gently simmering water. Stir until the chocolate is just melted then remove from the heat. Beat until smooth and leave the mixture to cool. When cool enough to handle, knead to a smooth paste on a clean work surface. The mixture can now be rolled and cut to shape. If the paste hardens, wrap it in clingfilm and warm it in the microwave for a few seconds on low.

Caramel and Praline Decorations

CARAMEL Put 75 g/3 oz of granulated sugar into a heavy-based saucepan with about 3 tablespoons of cold water. Over a low heat, stir well until the sugar has dissolved completely. If any sugar clings to the pan, brush it down using a wet brush. Bring the mixture to the boil and cook, without stirring, until the mixture turns golden. You may need to tilt the pan carefully to ensure the sugar colours evenly. As soon as the desired colour is reached, remove the pan from the heat and

CARAMEL SHAPES Make the caramel, remove the pan from the heat and plunge into cold water as described earlier. Using a teaspoon, drizzle or pour spoonfuls of caramel on to an oiled baking sheet. Leave to set before removing from the tray. Do not refrigerate caramel shapes as they will liquefy.

CARAMEL LACE Follow the method for caramel shapes, but use the teaspoon to drizzle threads in a random pattern on to an oiled tray. When set, break into pieces to use as decorations. Do not refrigerate.

Biscuits & Cookies

Cantuccini

MAKES 24 BISCUITS

250 g/9 oz plain flour
250 g/9 oz caster sugar
½ tsp baking powder
½ tsp vanilla essence
2 medium eggs

1 medium egg yolk
100 g/3½ oz mixed almonds
    and hazelnuts, toasted
    and roughly chopped
1 tsp whole aniseed

1 medium egg yolk mixed
    with 1 tbsp water, to glaze
Vin Santo or coffee, to serve

Preheat oven to 180°C/350°F/Gas Mark 4. Line a large baking sheet with non-stick baking parchment. Place the flour, caster sugar, baking powder, vanilla essence, the whole eggs and one of the egg yolks into a food processor and blend until the mixture forms a ball, scraping down the sides once or twice. Turn the mixture out on to a lightly floured surface and knead in the chopped nuts and aniseed.

Divide the paste into 3 pieces and roll into logs about 4 cm/1½ inches wide. Place the logs on to the baking sheet at least 5 cm/2 inches apart. Brush lightly with the other egg yolk beaten with 1 tablespoon of water and bake in the preheated oven for 30–35 minutes.

Remove from the oven and reduce the oven temperature to 150°C/300°F/Gas Mark 2. Cut the logs diagonally into 2.5 cm/ 1 inch slices and lay cut-side down on the baking sheet. Return to the oven for a further 30–40 minutes, or until dry and firm. Cool on a wire rack and store in an airtight container. Serve with Vin Santo or coffee.

Try this: FOR AN ALTERNATIVE: 32 FOR A CAKE: 222

Almond & Pistachio Biscotti

MAKES 12 BISCUITS

125 g/4 oz ground almonds
50 g/2 oz shelled pistachios
50 g/2 oz blanched almonds
2 medium eggs

1 medium egg yolk
125 g/4 oz icing sugar
225 g/8 oz plain flour
1 tsp baking powder

pinch of salt
zest of ½ lemon

Preheat oven to 180°C/350°F/Gas Mark 4. Line a large baking sheet with non-stick baking parchment. Toast the ground almonds and whole nuts lightly and reserve until cool.

Beat together the eggs, egg yolk and icing sugar until thick, then beat in the flour, baking powder and salt. Add the lemon zest, ground almonds and whole nuts and mix to form a slightly sticky dough.

Turn the dough on to a lightly floured surface and, using lightly floured hands, form into a log measuring approximately 30 cm/12 inches long. Place down the centre of the prepared baking sheet and transfer to the preheated oven. Bake for 20 minutes.

Remove from the oven and increase the oven temperature to 200°C/400°F/Gas Mark 6. Cut the log diagonally into 2.5 cm/1 inch slices. Return to the baking sheet, cut-side down and bake for a further 10–15 minutes until golden, turning once after 10 minutes. Leave to cool on a wire rack and store in an airtight container.

Try this: FOR AN ALTERNATIVE: 34 FOR A CAKE: 204

Italian Biscotti

MAKES 26–28 BISCUITS

150 g/5 oz butter
200 g/7 oz caster sugar
¼ tsp vanilla essence

1 small egg, beaten
¼ tsp ground cinnamon
grated rind of 1 lemon

15 g/ ½ oz ground almonds
150 g/5 oz plain flour
150 g/5 oz plain dark chocolate

Preheat the oven to 190°C/375°F/Gas Mark 5, 10 minutes before baking. Lightly oil 3–4 baking sheets and reserve. Cream the butter and sugar together in a bowl and mix in the vanilla essence. When it is light and fluffy beat in the egg with the cinnamon, lemon rind and the ground almonds. Stir in the flour to make a firm dough.

Knead lightly until smooth and free from cracks. Shape the dough into rectangular blocks about 4 cm/1½ inches in diameter, wrap in greaseproof paper and chill in the refrigerator for at least 2 hours.

Cut the chilled dough into 5 mm/¼ inch slices, place on the baking sheets and cook in the preheated oven for 12–15 minutes or until firm. Remove from the oven, cool slightly, then transfer to wire racks to cool.

When completely cold, melt the chocolate in a heatproof bowl set over a saucepan of simmering water. Alternatively, melt the chocolate in the microwave according to the manufacturer's instructions. Spoon into a piping bag and pipe over the biscuits. Leave to dry on a sheet of nonstick baking parchment before serving.

Try this: FOR AN ALTERNATIVE: 32   FOR A CAKE: 220

Chocolate Chip Cookies

MAKES ABOUT 30

140 g/4½ oz butter
50 g/2 oz caster sugar
60 g/2½ oz soft dark
    brown sugar

1 medium egg, beaten
½ tsp vanilla essence
125 g/4 oz plain flour
½ tsp bicarbonate of soda

150 g/5 oz plain or milk
    chocolate chips

Preheat the oven to 180˚C/350˚F/Gas Mark 4, 10 minutes before baking. Lightly butter 3–4 large baking sheets with 15 g/½ oz of the butter. Place the remaining butter and both sugars in a food processor and blend until smooth. Add the egg and vanilla essence and blend briefly. Alternatively, cream the butter and sugars together in a bowl, then beat in the egg with the vanilla essence.

If using a food processor, scrape out the mixture with a spatula and place the mixture into a large bowl. Sift the flour and bicarbonate of soda together, then fold into the creamed mixture. When the mixture is blended thoroughly, stir in the chocolate chips.

Drop heaped teaspoons of the mixture onto the prepared baking sheets, spaced well apart, and bake the cookies in the preheated oven for 10–12 minutes or until lightly golden.

Leave to cool for a few seconds, then using a spatula, transfer to a wire rack and cool completely. The cookies are best eaten when just cooked, but can be stored in an airtight tin for a few days.

 Try this: FOR AN ALTERNATIVE: 38 FOR A CAKE: 278

Chocolate Chip Cookies Variation

MAKES 36 BISCUITS

175 g/6 oz plain flour	¼ tsp bicarbonate of soda	brown sugar
pinch of salt	75 g/3 oz butter or margarine	3 tbsp golden syrup
1 tsp baking powder	50 g/2 oz soft light	125 g/4 oz chocolate chips

Preheat the oven to 190°C/375°F/Gas Mark 5, 10 minutes before baking. Lightly oil a large baking sheet.

In a large bowl, sift together the flour, salt, baking powder and bicarbonate of soda. Cut the butter or margarine into small pieces and add to the flour mixture.

Using 2 knives or the fingertips, rub in the butter or margarine until the mixture resembles coarse breadcrumbs. Add the light brown sugar, golden syrup and chocolate chips. Mix together until a smooth dough forms.

Shape the mixture into small balls and arrange on the baking sheet, leaving enough space to allow them to expand. (These cookies do not increase in size by a great deal, but allow a little space for expansion.)

Flatten the mixture slightly with the fingertips or the heel of the hand. Bake in the preheated oven for 12–15 minutes, or until golden and cooked through.

Allow to cool slightly, then transfer the biscuits on to a wire rack to cool. Serve when cold or otherwise store in an airtight tin.

Try this: FOR AN ALTERNATIVE: 36   FOR A CAKE: 294

Chewy Choc & Nut Cookies

MAKES 18

15 g/½ oz butter
4 medium egg whites
350 g/12 oz icing sugar

75 g/3 oz cocoa powder
2 tbsp plain flour
1 tsp instant coffee powder

125 g/4 oz walnuts,
finely chopped

Preheat the oven to 180°C/350°F/Gas Mark 4, 10 minutes before baking. Lightly butter several baking sheets with the butter and line with a sheet of non-stick baking parchment.

Place the egg whites in a large grease-free bowl and whisk with an electric mixer until the egg whites are very frothy. Add the sugar along with the cocoa powder, flour and coffee powder and whisk again until the ingredients are blended thoroughly. Add 1 tablespoon of water and continue to whisk on the highest speed until the mixture is very thick. Fold in the chopped walnuts.

Place tablespoons of the mixture onto the prepared baking sheets, leaving plenty of space between them as they expand greatly during cooking.

Bake in the preheated oven for 12–15 minutes, or until the tops are firm and quite cracked. Leave to cool for 30 seconds, then using a spatula, transfer to a wire rack and leave to cool. Store in an airtight tin.

Try this: FOR AN ALTERNATIVE: 70 FOR A CAKE: 92

Peanut Butter Truffle Cookies

MAKES 18

125 g/4 oz plain dark
  chocolate
150 ml/¼ pint double cream
125 g/4 oz butter or

margarine, softened
125 g/4 oz caster sugar
125 g/4 oz crunchy or
  smooth peanut butter

4 tbsp golden syrup
1 tbsp milk
225 g/8 oz plain flour
½ tsp bicarbonate of soda

Preheat the oven to 180°C/350°F/Gas Mark 4, 10 minutes before baking. Make the chocolate filling by breaking the chocolate into small pieces and placing in a heatproof bowl. Put the double cream into a saucepan and heat to boiling point. Immediately pour over the chocolate. Leave to stand for 1–2 minutes, then stir until smooth. Set aside to cool until firm enough to scoop. Do not refrigerate.

Lightly oil a baking sheet. Cream together the butter or margarine and the sugar until light and fluffy. Blend in the peanut butter, followed by the golden syrup and milk.

Sift together the flour and bicarbonate of soda. Add to the peanut butter mixture, mix well and knead until smooth.

Flatten 1–2 tablespoons of the cookie mixture on a chopping board. Put a spoonful of the chocolate mixture into the centre of the cookie dough, then fold the dough around the chocolate to enclose completely.

Put the balls on to the baking sheet and flatten slightly. Bake in the preheated oven for 10–12 minutes until golden. Remove from the oven and transfer to a wire rack to cool completely and serve.

Try this: FOR AN ALTERNATIVE: 96 FOR A CAKE: 284

White Chocolate Cookies

MAKES ABOUT 24

140 g/4½ oz butter
40 g/1½ oz caster sugar
60 g/2½ oz soft dark
   brown sugar

1 medium egg
125 g/4 oz plain flour
½ tsp bicarbonate of soda
few drops of vanilla essence

150 g/5 oz white chocolate
50 g/2 oz whole
   hazelnuts, shelled

Preheat the oven to 180°C/350°F/Gas Mark 4, 10 minutes before baking. Lightly butter several baking sheets with 15 g/½ oz of the butter.

Place the remaining butter with both sugars into a large bowl and beat with a wooden spoon or an electric mixer until soft and fluffy. Beat the egg, then gradually beat into the creamed mixture. Sift the flour and the bicarbonate of soda together, then carefully fold into the creamed mixture with a few drops of vanilla essence.

Roughly chop the chocolate and hazelnuts into small pieces, add to the bowl and gently stir into the mixture. Mix together lightly to blend.

Spoon heaped teaspoons of the mixture onto the prepared baking sheets, making sure that there is plenty of space in between each one as they will spread a lot during cooking.

Bake the cookies in the preheated oven for 10 minutes or until golden, then remove from the oven and leave to cool for 1 minute. Using a spatula, carefully transfer to a wire rack and leave to cool completely. The cookies are best eaten on the day they are made. Store in an airtight tin.

Try this: FOR AN ALTERNATIVE: 140   FOR A CAKE: 244

Oatmeal Raisin Cookies

MAKES 24

175 g/6 oz plain flour
150 g/5 oz rolled oats
1 tsp ground ginger
½ tsp baking powder
½ tsp bicarbonate of soda

125 g/4 oz soft
   light brown sugar
50 g/2 oz raisins
1 medium egg,
   lightly beaten

150 ml/¼ pint vegetable
   or sunflower oil
4 tbsp milk

Preheat the oven to 200°C/400°F/Gas Mark 6, 15 minutes before baking. Lightly oil a baking sheet.

Mix together the flour, oats, ground ginger, baking powder, bicarbonate of soda, sugar and the raisins in a large bowl.

In another bowl, mix the egg, oil and milk together. Make a well in the centre of the dry ingredients and pour in the egg mixture.

Mix the mixture together well with either a fork or a wooden spoon to make a soft but not sticky dough.

Place spoonfuls of the dough well apart on the oiled baking sheet and flatten the tops down slightly with the tines of a fork. Transfer the biscuits to the preheated oven and bake for 10–12 minutes until golden.

Remove from the oven, leave to cool for 2–3 minutes, then transfer the biscuits to a wire rack to cool. Serve when cold, or otherwise store in an airtight tin.

Try this: FOR AN ALTERNATIVE: 48 FOR A CAKE: 168

Oatmeal Coconut Cookies

MAKES 40

225 g/8 oz butter
   or margarine
125 g/4 oz soft light
   brown sugar

125 g/4 oz caster sugar
1 large egg, lightly beaten
1 tsp vanilla essence
225 g/8 oz plain flour

1 tsp baking powder
½ tsp bicarbonate of soda
125 g/4 oz rolled oats
75 g/3 oz desiccated coconut

Preheat the oven to 180°C/350°F/Gas Mark 4, 10 minutes before baking. Lightly oil a baking sheet.

Cream together the butter or margarine and sugars until light and fluffy. Gradually stir in the egg and vanilla essence and beat until well blended.

Sift together the flour, baking powder and bicarbonate of soda in another bowl. Add to the butter and sugar mixture and beat together until smooth. Fold in the rolled oats and coconut with a metal spoon or rubber spatula.

Roll heaped teaspoonfuls of the mixture into balls and place on the baking sheet about 5 cm/2 inches apart and flatten each ball slightly with the heel of the hand.

Transfer to the preheated oven and bake for 12–15 minutes, until just golden.

Remove from the oven and transfer the biscuits to wire rack to cool completely before serving.

Try this: FOR AN ALTERNATIVE: 46 FOR A CAKE: 212

Pumpkin Cookies with Brown Butter Glaze

MAKES 48

125 g/4 oz butter, softened
150 g/5 oz plain flour
175 g/6 oz soft light brown
   sugar, lightly packed
225 g/8 oz canned pumpkin
   or cooked pumpkin
1 medium egg, beaten

2 tsp ground cinnamon
2½ tsp vanilla essence
½ tsp baking powder
½ tsp bicarbonate of soda
½ tsp freshly grated nutmeg
125 g/4 oz wholemeal flour
75 g/3 oz pecans,

   roughly chopped
100 g/3½ oz raisins
50 g/2 oz unsalted butter
225 g/8 oz icing sugar
2 tbsp milk

Preheat the oven to 190°C/375°F/Gas Mark 5, 10 minutes before baking. Lightly oil a baking sheet and reserve.

Using an electric mixer, beat the butter until light and fluffy. Add the flour, sugar, pumpkin, beaten egg and beat with the mixer until mixed well.

Stir in the ground cinnamon, 1 teaspoon of the vanilla essence and then sift in the baking powder, bicarbonate of soda and grated nutmeg. Beat the mixture until combined well, scraping down the sides of the bowl.

Add the wholemeal flour, chopped nuts and raisins to the mixture and fold in with a metal spoon or rubber spatula until mixed thoroughly together. Place teaspoonfuls about 5 cm/ 2 inches apart on to the baking sheet. Bake in the pre-heated oven for 10–12 minutes, or until the cookie edges are firm.

Remove the biscuits from the oven and leave to cool on a wire rack. Meanwhile, melt the butter in a small saucepan over a medium heat, until pale and just turning golden brown. Remove from the heat. Add the sugar, remaining vanilla essence and milk, stirring. Drizzle over the cooled cookies and serve.

Try this: FOR AN ALTERNATIVE: 52   FOR A CAKE: 228

Spiced Palmier Biscuits with Apple Purée

MAKES 20

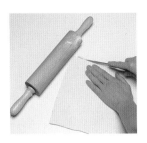

250 g/9 oz prepared puff pastry, thawed if frozen
40 g/1½ oz caster sugar
25 g/1 oz icing sugar
1 tsp ground cinnamon

¼ tsp ground ginger
¼ tsp freshly grated nutmeg
450 g/1 lb Bramley cooking apples, roughly chopped
50 g/2 oz sugar

25 g/1 oz raisins
25 g/1 oz dried cherries
zest of 1 orange
double cream, lightly whipped, to serve

Preheat the oven to 200°C/400°F/Gas Mark 6, 15 minutes before baking. Roll out the pastry on a lightly floured surface to form a 25.5 x 30.5 cm/10 x 12 inch rectangle. Trim the edges with a small sharp knife.

Sift together the caster sugar, icing sugar, cinnamon, ginger and nutmeg into a bowl. Generously dust both sides of the pastry sheet with about a quarter of the sugar mixture. With a long edge facing the body, fold either side halfway towards the centre. Dust with a third of the remaining sugar mixture. Fold each side again so that they almost meet in the centre and dust again with about half the remaining sugar mixture. Fold the two sides together down the centre of the pastry to give six layers altogether. Wrap the pastry in clingfilm and refrigerate for 1–2 hours until firm. Reserve the remaining spiced sugar.

Remove the pastry from the refrigerator, unwrap and roll in the remaining sugar to give a good coating all round. Using a sharp knife, cut the roll into about 20 thin slices. Place the cut side down on to a baking sheet and place in the pre-heated oven. Cook for 10 minutes, turn the biscuits over and cook for a further 5–10 minutes, or until golden and crisp. Remove from the oven and transfer to a wire rack. Allow to cool completely.

Meanwhile, combine the remaining ingredients in a saucepan. Cover and cook gently for 15 minutes until the apple is completely soft. Stir well and allow to cool. Serve the palmiers with a spoonful of the apple purée and a little of the whipped double cream

Try this: FOR AN ALTERNATIVE: 86   FOR A CAKE: 180

Whipped Shortbread

MAKES 36

225 g/8 oz butter, softened
75 g/3 oz icing sugar
175 g/6 oz plain flour

hundreds and thousands
sugar strands
chocolate drops

silver balls
50 g/2 oz icing sugar
2–3 tsp lemon juice

Preheat the oven to 180°C/350°F/Gas Mark 4, 10 minutes before baking. Lightly oil a baking sheet.

Cream the butter and icing sugar until fluffy. Gradually add the flour and continue beating for a further 2–3 minutes until it is smooth and light.

Roll into balls and place on a baking sheet. Cover half of the dough mixture with hundreds and thousands, sugar strands, chocolate drops or silver balls. Keep the other half plain.

Bake in the preheated oven for 6–8 minutes, until the bottoms are lightly browned. Remove from the oven and transfer to a wire rack to cool.

Sift the icing sugar into a small bowl. Add the lemon juice and blend until a smooth icing forms.

Using a small spoon, swirl the icing over the cooled plain cookies. Decorate with either the extra hundreds and thousands, chocolate drops or silver balls and serve.

Try this: FOR AN ALTERNATIVE: 74 FOR A CAKE: 194

Chocolate Shortcake

MAKES 30-32

225 g/8 oz unsalted butter, softened	1 tsp vanilla essence	¼ tsp salt
150 g/5 oz icing sugar	250 g/9 oz plain flour	extra icing sugar, to decorate
	25 g/1 oz cocoa powder	

Preheat the oven to 170°C/325°F/Gas Mark 3, 10 minutes before baking. Lightly oil several baking sheets and line with non-stick baking parchment. Place the butter, icing sugar and vanilla essence together in a food processor and blend briefly until smooth. Alternatively, using a wooden spoon, cream the butter, icing sugar and vanilla essence in a large bowl.

Sift the flour, cocoa powder and salt together then either add to the food processor bowl and blend quickly to form a dough, or add to the bowl and, using your hands, mix together until a smooth dough is formed.

Turn the dough out onto a clean board lined with clingfilm. Place another sheet of clingfilm over the top and roll the dough out until it is 1 cm/½ inch thick. Transfer the whole board to the refrigerator and chill for 1½–2 hours.

Remove the top piece of clingfilm and use a 5 cm/2 inch cutter to cut the dough into 30–32 rounds. Place the rounds on the prepared baking sheets and bake in the preheated oven for about 15 minutes or until firm.

Cool for 1 minute, then using a spatula, carefully remove the shortcakes from the baking parchment and transfer to a wire rack. Leave to cool completely. Sprinkle the shortcakes with sifted icing sugar before serving. Store in an airtight tin for a few days.

Try this: FOR AN ALTERNATIVE: 72 FOR A CAKE: 276

Chocolate Macaroons

MAKES 20

650 g/2½ oz plain
   dark chocolate
125 g/4 oz ground almonds

125 g/4 oz caster sugar
¼ tsp almond essence
1 tbsp cocoa powder

2 medium egg whites
1 tbsp icing sugar

Preheat the oven to 180°C/350°F/Gas Mark 4, 10 minutes before baking. Lightly oil several baking sheets and line with sheets of non-stick baking parchment. Melt the chocolate in a heatproof bowl set over a saucepan of simmering water. Alternatively, melt in the microwave according to the manufacturer's instructions. Stir until smooth, then cool slightly.

Place the ground almonds in a food processor and add the sugar, almond essence, cocoa powder and 1 of the egg whites. Add the melted chocolate and a little of the other egg white and blend to make a soft, smooth paste. Alternatively, place the ground almonds with the sugar, almond essence and cocoa powder in a bowl and make a well in the centre. Add the melted chocolate with sufficient egg white and gradually blend together to form a smooth but not sticky paste.

Shape the dough into small balls the size of large walnuts and place them on the prepared baking sheets. Flatten them slightly, then brush with a little water. Sprinkle over a little icing sugar and bake in the preheated oven for 10–12 minutes or until just firm.

Using a spatula, carefully lift the macaroons off the baking parchment and transfer to a wire rack to cool. These are best served immediately, but can be stored in an airtight container.

Try this: FOR AN ALTERNATIVE: 60 FOR A CAKE: 292

Almond Macaroons

MAKES 12

rice paper
125 g/4 oz caster sugar
50 g/2 oz ground almonds

1 tsp ground rice
2–3 drops almond essence
1 medium egg white

8 blanched almonds,
halved

Preheat the oven to 150°C/300°F/Gas Mark 2, 10 minutes before baking. Line a baking sheet with the rice paper.

Mix the caster sugar, ground almonds, ground rice and almond essence together and reserve.

Whisk the egg white until stiff then gently fold in the caster sugar mixture with a metal spoon or rubber spatula.

Mix to form a stiff but not sticky paste. If the mixture is very sticky, add a little extra ground almonds. Place small spoonfuls of the mixture, about the size of an apricot, well apart on the rice paper.

Place a half-blanched almond in the centre of each. Place in the preheated oven and bake for 25 minutes,or until just pale golden.

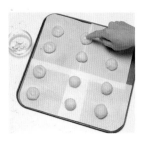

Remove the biscuits from the oven and leave to cool for a few minutes on the baking sheet. Cut or tear the rice paper around the macaroons to release them. Once cold, serve them or store in an airtight tin.

Ginger Snaps

MAKES 40

300 g/11 oz butter or margarine, softened
225 g/8 oz soft light brown sugar
75 g/3 oz black treacle

1 medium egg
400 g/14 oz plain flour
2 tsp bicarbonate of soda
½ tsp salt
1 tsp ground ginger

1 tsp ground cloves
1 tsp ground cinnamon
50 g/2 oz granulated sugar

Preheat the oven to 190°C/375°F/Gas Mark 5, 10 minutes before baking. Lightly oil a baking sheet.

Cream together the butter or margarine and the sugar until light and fluffy.

Warm the treacle in the microwave for 30–40 seconds, then add gradually to the butter mixture with the egg. Beat until combined well.

In a separate bowl, sift the flour, bicarbonate of soda, salt, ground ginger, ground cloves and ground cinnamon. Add to the butter mixture and mix together to form a firm dough.

Chill in the refrigerator for 1 hour. Shape the dough into small balls and roll in the granulated sugar. Place well apart on the oiled baking sheet.

Sprinkle the baking sheet with a little water and transfer to the preheated oven.

Bake for 12 minutes, until golden and crisp. Transfer to a wire rack to cool and serve.

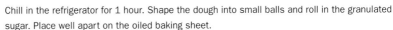

Try this: FOR AN ALTERNATIVE: 64 FOR A CAKE: 210

Chocolate & Ginger Florentines

MAKES 14–16

40 g/1½ oz butter
5 tbsp double cream
50 g/2 oz caster sugar
60 g/2½ oz chopped almonds

25 g/1 oz flaked almonds
40 g/1½ oz glacé
   ginger, chopped
25 g/1 oz plain flour

pinch of salt
150 g/5 oz plain
   dark chocolate

Preheat the oven to 180°C/350°F/Gas Mark 4, 10 minutes before baking. Lightly oil several baking sheets.

Melt the butter, cream and sugar together in a saucepan and bring slowly to the boil. Remove from the heat and stir in the almonds and the glacé ginger.

Leave to cool slightly, then mix in the flour and the salt. Blend together, then place heaped teaspoons of the mixture on the baking sheets. Make sure they are spaced well apart as they expand during cooking. Flatten them slightly with the back of a wet spoon.

Bake in the preheated oven for 10–12 minutes or until just brown at the edges. Leave to cool slightly. Using a spatula, carefully transfer to a wire rack and leave to cool.

Melt the chocolate in a heatproof bowl set over a saucepan of gently simmering water. Alternatively, melt the chocolate in the microwave according to the manufacturer's instructions, until just liquid and smooth. Spread thickly over one side of the Florentines, then mark wavy lines through the chocolate using a fork and leave until firm.

Try this: FOR AN ALTERNATIVE: 62 FOR A CAKE: 156

Chocolate & Nut
Refrigerator Biscuits

MAKES 18

165 g/5½ oz slightly
  salted butter
150 g/5 oz soft dark
  brown sugar

25 g/1 oz granulated sugar
1 medium egg, beaten
200 g/7 oz plain flour
½ tsp bicarbonate of soda

25 g/1 oz cocoa powder
125 g/4 oz pecan nuts,
  finely chopped

Preheat the oven to 190°C/375°F/Gas Mark 5, 10 minutes before baking. Lightly grease several baking sheets with 15 g/½ oz of the butter. Cream the remaining butter and both sugars in a large bowl until light and fluffy, then gradually beat in the egg.

Sift the flour, bicarbonate of soda and cocoa powder together then gradually fold into the creamed mixture together with the chopped pecans. Mix thoroughly until a smooth but stiff dough is formed.

Place the dough on a lightly floured surface or pastry board and roll into sausage shapes about 5 cm/2 inches in diameter. Wrap in clingfilm and chill in the refrigerator for at least 12 hours, or preferably overnight.

Cut the dough into thin slices and place on the prepared baking sheets. Bake in the preheated oven for 8–10 minutes or until firm. Remove from the oven and leave to cool slightly. Using a spatula, transfer to a wire rack to cool. Store in an airtight tin.

Try this: FOR AN ALTERNATIVE: 40 FOR A CAKE: 262

Chocolate Florentines

MAKES 20

125 g/4 oz butter or margarine
125 g/4 oz soft light
   brown sugar
1 tbsp double cream
50 g/2 oz blanched almonds,
   roughly chopped

50 g/2 oz hazelnuts,
   roughly chopped
75 g/3 oz sultanas
50 g/2 oz glacé cherries,
   roughly chopped
50 g/2 oz plain, dark

chocolate, roughly
   chopped or broken
50 g/2 oz milk chocolate,
   roughly chopped or broken
50 g/2 oz white chocolate,
   roughly chopped or broken

Preheat the oven to 180°C/350°F/Gas Mark 4, 10 minutes before baking. Lightly oil a baking sheet.

Melt the butter or margarine with the sugar and double cream in a small saucepan over a very low heat. Do not boil. Remove from the heat and stir in the almonds, hazelnuts, sultanas and cherries.

Drop teaspoonfuls of the mixture on to the baking sheet. Transfer to the preheated oven and bake for 10 minutes, until golden. Leave the biscuits to cool on the baking sheet for about 5 minutes, then carefully transfer to a wire rack to cool.

Melt the plain, milk and white chocolates in separate bowls, either in the microwave following the manufacturer's instructions or in a small bowl, placed over a saucepan of gently simmering water.

Spread one third of the biscuits with the plain chocolate, one third with the milk chocolate and one third with the white chocolate. Mark out wavy lines on the chocolate when almost set with the tines of a fork. Alternatively, dip some of the biscuits in chocolate to half coat and serve.

Try this: FOR AN ALTERNATIVE: 64   FOR A CAKE: 238

Chocolate & Hazelnut Cookies

MAKES 12

75 g/3 oz blanched hazelnuts	5 tsp cocoa powder	2 tbsp rum
100 g/3½ oz caster sugar	3 tbsp double cream	75 g/3 oz white chocolate
50 g/2 oz unsalted butter	2 large egg whites	
pinch of salt	40 g/1½ oz plain flour	

Preheat the oven to 180°C/350°F/Gas Mark 4, 10 minutes before baking. Lightly oil and flour 2–3 baking sheets. Chop 25 g/1 oz of the hazelnuts and reserve. Blend the remaining hazelnuts with the caster sugar in a food processor until finely ground. Add the butter to the processor bowl and blend until pale and creamy.

Add the salt, cocoa powder and the double cream and mix well. Scrape the mixture into a bowl, using a spatula, and stir in the egg whites. Sift the flour, then stir into the mixture together with the rum.

Spoon heaped tablespoons of the batter onto the baking sheets and sprinkle over a few of the reserved hazelnuts. Bake in the preheated oven for 5–7 minutes or until firm. Remove the cookies from the oven and leave to cool for 1–2 minutes. Using a spatula, transfer to wire racks and leave to cool.

When the biscuits are cold, melt the chocolate in a heatproof bowl set over a saucepan of simmering water. Stir until smooth, then drizzle a little of the chocolate over the top of each biscuit. Leave to dry on a wire rack before serving.

Try this: FOR AN ALTERNATIVE: 66   FOR A CAKE: 240

Chocolate & Almond Biscuits

MAKES 18-20

140 g/4½ oz butter
60 g/2½ oz icing sugar
1 medium egg, beaten
1 tbsp milk

grated rind of 1 lemon
250 g/9 oz plain flour
100 g/3½ oz blanched
    almonds, chopped

125 g/4 oz plain
    dark chocolate
75 g/3 oz flaked
    almonds, toasted

Preheat the oven to 200°C/400°F/Gas Mark 6, 15 minutes before baking. Lightly oil several baking sheets.

Cream the butter and icing sugar together until light and fluffy, then gradually beat in the egg, beating well after each addition. When all the egg has been added, stir in the milk and lemon rind. Sift the flour then stir into the mixture together with the chopped almonds to form a smooth and pliable dough. Wrap in clingfilm and chill in the refrigerator for 2 hours.

Roll the dough out on a lightly floured surface, in a large oblong about 5 mm/¼ inch thick. Cut into strips, about 6.5 cm/2½ inches long and 4 cm/1½ inches wide and place on the prepared baking sheets.

Bake in the preheated oven for 15 minutes, or until golden, then remove from the oven and leave to cool for a few minutes. Transfer to a wire rack and leave to cool completely.

Melt the chocolate in a heatproof bowl set over a saucepan of simmering water. Alternatively, the chocolate can be melted in the microwave according to the manufacturer's instructions, until smooth. Spread the chocolate thickly over the biscuits, sprinkle over the toasted flaked almonds and leave to set before serving.

Try this: FOR AN ALTERNATIVE: 60 FOR A CAKE: 242

Shortbread Thumbs

MAKES 12

125 g/4 oz self-raising flour
125 g/4 oz butter, softened
25 g/1 oz white vegetable fat
50 g/2 oz granulated sugar

25 g/1 oz cornflour, sifted
5 tbsp cocoa powder, sifted
125 g/4 oz icing sugar
6 assorted coloured glacé

cherries, rinsed, dried
and halved

Preheat the oven to 150˚C/300˚F/Gas Mark 2, 10 minutes before baking. Lightly oil 2 baking sheets. Sift the flour into a large bowl, cut 75 g/3 oz of the butter and the white vegetable fat into small cubes, add to the flour, then, using your fingertips, rub in until the mixture resembles fine breadcrumbs.

Stir in the granulated sugar, sifted cornflour and 4 tablespoons of cocoa powder and bring the mixture together with your hand to form a soft and pliable dough.

Place on a lightly floured surface and shape into 12 small balls. Place onto the baking sheets at least 5 cm/2 inches apart, then press each one with a clean thumb to make a dent.

Bake in the preheated oven for 20–25 minutes or until light golden brown. Remove from the oven and leave for 1–2 minutes to cool. Transfer to a wire rack and leave until cold.

Sift the icing sugar and the remaining cocoa powder into a bowl and add the remaining softened butter. Blend to form a smooth and spreadable icing with 1–2 tablespoons of hot water. Spread a little icing over the top of each biscuit and place half a cherry on each. Leave until set before serving.

Try this: FOR AN ALTERNATIVE: 56 FOR A CAKE: 146

Chequered Biscuits

MAKES 20

150 g/5 oz butter	pinch of salt	25 g/1 oz cocoa powder
75 g/3 oz icing sugar	200 g/7 oz plain flour	1 small egg white

Preheat the oven to 190°C/375°F/Gas Mark 5, 10 minutes before baking. Lightly oil 3–4 baking sheets. Place the butter and icing sugar in a bowl and cream together until light and fluffy.

Add the salt, then gradually add the flour, beating well after each addition. Mix well to form a firm dough. Cut the dough in half and knead the cocoa powder into one half. Wrap both portions of dough separately in clingfilm and then leave to chill in the refrigerator for 2 hours.

Divide each piece of dough into 3 portions. Roll each portion of dough into a long roll and arrange these rolls on top of each other to form a chequerboard design, sealing them with egg white. Wrap in clingfilm and refrigerate for 1 hour.

Cut the dough into 5 mm/¼ inch thick slices, place on the baking sheets and bake in the preheated oven for 10–15 minutes. Remove from the oven, and leave to cool for a few minutes. Transfer to a wire rack and leave until cold before serving. Store in an airtight tin.

Try this: FOR AN ALTERNATIVE: 80 FOR A CAKE: 266

Coconut & Almond Munchies

MAKES 26-30

5 medium egg whites
250 g/9 oz icing sugar, plus
　extra to sprinkle

225 g/8 oz ground almonds
200 g/7 oz desiccated coconut
grated rind of 1 lemon

125 g/4 oz milk chocolate
125 g/4 oz white chocolate

Preheat the oven to 150°C/300°F/Gas Mark 2, 10 minutes before baking. Line several baking sheets with rice paper. Place the egg whites in a clean, grease-free bowl and whisk until stiff and standing in peaks. Sift the icing sugar, then carefully fold half of the sugar into the whisked egg whites together with the ground almonds. Add the coconut, the remaining icing sugar and the lemon rind and mix together to form a very sticky dough.

Place the mixture in a piping bag and pipe the mixture into walnut-sized mounds onto the rice paper, then sprinkle with a little extra icing sugar. Bake in the preheated oven for 20–25 minutes, or until set and golden on the outside. Remove from the oven and leave to cool slightly. Using a spatula, carefully transfer to a wire rack and leave until cold.

Break the milk and white chocolate into pieces and place in two separate bowls. Melt both chocolates set over saucepans of gently simmering water. Alternatively, melt in the microwave, according to the manufacturer's instructions. Stir until smooth and free from lumps. Dip one edge of each munchie in the milk chocolate and leave to dry on non-stick baking parchment. When dry, dip the other side into the white chocolate. Leave to set, then serve as soon as possible.

Try this: FOR AN ALTERNATIVE: 48 FOR A CAKE: 252

Honey & Chocolate Hearts

MAKES ABOUT 20

60 g/2½ oz caster sugar
15 g/½ oz butter
125 g/4 oz thick honey
1 small egg, beaten

pinch of salt
1 tbsp mixed peel or
   chopped glacé ginger
¼ tsp ground cinnamon

pinch of ground cloves
225 g/8 oz plain flour, sifted
½ tsp baking powder, sifted
75 g/3 oz milk chocolate

Preheat the oven to 220°C/425°F/Gas Mark 7, 15 minutes before baking. Lightly oil two baking sheets. Heat the sugar, butter and honey together in a small saucepan until everything has melted and the mixture is smooth.

Remove from the heat and stir until slightly cooled, then add the beaten egg with the salt and beat well. Stir in the mixed peel or glacé ginger, ground cinnamon, ground cloves, the flour and the baking powder and mix well until a dough is formed. Wrap in clingfilm and chill in the refrigerator for 45 minutes.

Place the chilled dough on a lightly floured surface, roll out to about 5 mm/¼ inch thickness and cut out small heart shapes. Place onto the prepared baking sheets and bake in the preheated oven for 8–10 minutes. Remove from the oven and leave to cool slightly. Using a spatula, transfer to a wire rack until cold.

Melt the chocolate in a heatproof bowl set over a saucepan of simmering water. Alternatively, melt the chocolate in the microwave according to the manufacturer's instructions, until smooth. Dip one half of each biscuit in the melted chocolate. Leave to set before serving.

Try this: FOR AN ALTERNATIVE: 76 FOR A CAKE: 208

Chocolate Orange Biscuits

MAKES 30

100 g/3½ oz plain
   dark chocolate
125 g/4 oz butter
125 g/4 oz caster sugar

pinch of salt
1 medium egg, beaten
grated zest of 2 oranges
200 g/7 oz plain flour

1 tsp baking powder
125 g/4 oz icing sugar
1–2 tbsp orange juice

Preheat the oven to 200°C/400°F/Gas Mark 6, 15 minutes before baking. Lightly oil several baking sheets. Coarsely grate the chocolate and reserve. Beat the butter and sugar together until creamy. Add the salt, beaten egg and half the orange zest and beat again.

Sift the flour and baking powder, add to the bowl with the grated chocolate and beat to form a dough. Shape into a ball, wrap in clingfilm and chill in the refrigerator for 2 hours.

Roll the dough out on a lightly floured surface to 5 mm/¼ inch thickness and cut into 5 cm/ 2 inch rounds. Place the rounds on the prepared baking sheets, allowing room for expansion. Bake in the preheated oven for 10–12 minutes or until firm. Remove the biscuits from the oven and leave to cool slightly. Using a spatula, transfer to a wire rack and leave to cool.

Sift the icing sugar into a small bowl and stir in sufficient orange juice to make a smooth, spreadable icing. Spread the icing over the biscuits, leave until almost set, then sprinkle on the remaining grated orange zest before serving.

Try this: FOR AN ALTERNATIVE: 52   FOR KIDS: 216

Rum & Chocolate Squares

MAKES 14-16

125 g/4 oz butter
100 g/3½ oz caster sugar
pinch of salt

2 medium egg yolks
225 g/8 oz plain flour
50 g/2 oz cornflour

¼ tsp baking powder
2 tbsp cocoa powder
1 tbsp rum

Preheat the oven to 190°C/350°F/Gas Mark 5, 10 minutes before baking. Lightly oil several baking sheets. Cream the butter, sugar and salt together in a large bowl until light and fluffy. Add the egg yolks and beat well until smooth.

Sift together 175 g/6 oz of the flour, the cornflour and the baking powder, add to the mixture and mix well with a wooden spoon until a smooth and soft dough is formed.

Halve the dough and knead the cocoa powder into one half and the rum and the remaining plain flour into the other half. Place the two mixtures in two separate bowls, cover with clingfilm and chill in the refrigerator for 1 hour.

Roll out both pieces of dough separately on a well floured surface into two thin rectangles about 5 mm/¼ inch thick. Place one on top of the other, cut out squares approximately 5 cm/2 inch square and place on the prepared baking sheets.

Bake in the preheated oven, half with the chocolate uppermost and the other half, rum side up, for 10–12 minutes or until firm. Remove from the oven and leave to cool slightly. Using a spatula, transfer to a wire rack and leave to cool, then serve.

Try this: FOR AN ALTERNATIVE: 34 FOR A CAKE: 258

Chocolate Whirls

MAKES 20

125 g/4 oz soft margarine
75 g/3 oz unsalted
   butter, softened
75 g/3 oz icing sugar, sifted
75 g/3 oz plain dark

chocolate, melted
   and cooled
15 g/½ oz cornflour, sifted
125 g/4 oz plain flour
125 g/4 oz self-raising flour

For the buttercream:
125 g/4 oz unsalted
   butter, softened
½ tsp vanilla essence
225 g/8 oz icing sugar, sifted

Preheat the oven to 180°C/350°F/Gas Mark 4, 10 minutes before baking. Lightly oil two baking sheets.

Cream the margarine, butter and icing sugar together until the mixture is light and fluffy. Stir the chocolate until smooth, then beat into the creamed mixture. Stir in the cornflour. Sift the flours together, then gradually add to the creamed mixture, a little at a time, beating well between each addition. Beat until the consistency is smooth and stiff enough for piping.

Put the mixture in a piping bag fitted with a large star nozzle and pipe 40 small whirls onto the prepared baking sheets. Bake the whirls in the preheated oven for 12–15 minutes or until firm to the touch. Remove from the oven and leave to cool for about 2 minutes. Using a spatula, transfer the whirls to wire racks and leave to cool.

Meanwhile, make the buttercream. Cream the butter with the vanilla essence until soft. Gradually beat in the icing sugar and add a little cooled boiled water, if necessary, to give a smooth consistency. When the whirls are cold, pipe or spread on the prepared buttercream, sandwich together and serve.

Brownies & Traybakes

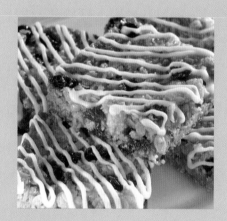

Chocolate Fudge Brownies

MAKES 16

125 g/4 oz butter	225 g/8 oz caster sugar	150 g/5 oz plain flour
175 g/6 oz plain dark	2 tsp vanilla essence	175 g/6 oz icing sugar
chocolate, roughly	2 medium eggs,	2 tbsp cocoa powder
chopped or broken	lightly beaten	15 g/½ oz butter

Preheat the oven to 180°C/350°F/Gas Mark 4, 10 minutes before baking. Lightly oil and line a 20.5 cm/8 inch square cake tin with greaseproof or baking paper.

Slowly melt the butter and chocolate together in a heatproof bowl set over a sauce-pan of simmering water. Transfer the mixture to a large bowl.

Stir in the sugar and vanilla essence, then stir in the eggs. Sift over the flour and fold together well with a metal spoon or rubber spatula. Pour into the prepared tin.

Transfer to the preheated oven and bake for 30 minutes until just set. Remove the cooked mixture from the oven and leave to cool in the tin before turning it out on to a wire rack.

Sift the icing sugar and cocoa powder into a small bowl and make a well in the centre. Place the butter in the well then gradually add about 2 tablespoons of hot water. Mix to form a smooth spreadable icing.

Pour the icing over the cooked mixture. Allow the icing to set before cutting into squares. Serve the brownies when they are cold.

Try this: FOR AN ALTERNATIVE: 94 FOR A CAKE: 216

Chocolate Nut Brownies

MAKES 16

125 g/4 oz butter
150 g/5 oz soft light brown
  sugar, firmly packed
50 g/2 oz plain dark
  chocolate, roughly
  chopped or broken

2 tbsp smooth peanut butter
2 medium eggs
50 g/2 oz unsalted roasted
  peanuts, finely chopped
100 g/3 ½ oz self-raising
  flour

For the topping:
125 g/4 oz plain dark
  chocolate, roughly
  chopped or broken
50 ml/2 fl oz soured cream

Preheat the oven to 180°C/350°F/Gas Mark 4, 10 minutes before baking. Lightly oil and line a 20.5 cm/8 inch square cake tin with greaseproof paper.

Combine the butter, sugar and chocolate in a small saucepan and heat gently until the sugar and chocolate have melted, stirring constantly. Reserve and cool slightly.

Mix together the peanut butter, eggs and peanuts in a large bowl. Stir in the cooled chocolate mixture. Sift in the flour and fold together with a metal spoon or rubber spatula until combined.

Pour into the prepared tin and bake in the preheated oven for about 30 minutes, or until just firm. Cool for 5 minutes in the tin before turning out on to a wire rack to cool.

To make the topping, melt the chocolate in a heatproof bowl over a saucepan of simmering water, making sure that the base of the bowl does not touch the water.

Cool slightly, then stir in the soured cream until smooth and glossy. Spread over the brownies, refrigerate until set, then cut into squares. Serve the brownies cold.

Try this: FOR AN ALTERNATIVE: 90 FOR A CAKE: 270

Triple Chocolate Brownies

MAKES 15

350 g/12 oz plain dark
   chocolate, broken
   into pieces
225 g/8 oz butter, cubed
225 g/8 oz caster sugar
3 large eggs, lightly beaten

1 tsp vanilla essence
2 tbsp very strong
   black coffee
100 g/3½ oz self-raising flour
125 g/4 oz pecans,
   roughly chopped

75 g/3 oz white chocolate,
   roughly chopped
75 g/3 oz milk chocolate,
   roughly chopped

Preheat the oven to 190°C/375°F/Gas Mark 5, 10 minutes before baking. Oil and line a 28 x 18 x 2.5 cm/11 x 7 x 1 inch cake tin with non-stick baking parchment.

Place the plain chocolate in a heatproof bowl with the butter set over a saucepan of almost boiling water, and stir occasionally until melted. Remove from the heat and leave until just cool, but not beginning to set.

Place the caster sugar, eggs, vanilla essence and coffee in a large bowl and beat together until smooth. Gradually beat in the chocolate mixture. Sift the flour into the chocolate mixture. Add the pecans and the white and milk chocolate and gently fold in until mixed thoroughly.

Spoon the mixture into the prepared tin and level the top. Bake on the centre shelf of the preheated oven for 45 minutes, or until just firm to the touch in the centre and crusty on top. Leave to cool in the tin, then turn out onto a wire rack. Trim off the crusty edges and cut into 15 squares. Store in an airtight container.

Try this: FOR AN ALTERNATIVE: 92   FOR A CAKE: 282

Fudgy Chocolate Bars

MAKES 14

25 g/1 oz glacé cherries	dark chocolate	150 g/5 oz digestive biscuits
60 g/2½ oz shelled hazelnuts	150 g/5 oz unsalted butter	1 tbsp icing sugar,
150 g/5 oz plain	¼ tsp salt	sifted, optional

Preheat the oven to 180°C/350°F/Gas Mark 4, 10 minutes before baking. Lightly oil a
18 cm/7 inch square tin and line the base with non-stick baking parchment. Rinse the glacé
cherries thoroughly, dry well on absorbent kitchen paper and reserve.

Place the nuts on a baking tray and roast in the preheated oven for 10 minutes, or until light
golden brown. Leave to cool slightly, then chop roughly and reserve.

Break the chocolate into small pieces and place with the butter and salt in the top of a double
boiler, or in a bowl set over a saucepan of gently simmering water. Heat gently, stirring, until
melted and smooth. Alternatively, melt the chocolate in the microwave, according to the
manufacturer's instructions.

Chop the biscuits into 5 mm/¼ inch pieces and cut the cherries in half. Add to the chocolate
mixture with the nuts and stir well. Spoon the mixture into the prepared tin and level the top.

Chill in the refrigerator for 30 minutes, remove from the tin, discard the baking parchment and
cut into 14 bars. Cover lightly, return to the refrigerator and keep chilled until ready to serve.
To serve, lightly sprinkle the bars with sifted icing sugar, if using. Store the bars covered in
the refrigerator.

Try this: FOR AN ALTERNATIVE: 136 FOR A CAKE: 288

Chocolate Biscuit Bars

SERVES 20

50 g/2 oz sultanas
3–4 tbsp brandy (optional)
100 g/3½ oz plain
    dark chocolate
125 g/4 oz unsalted butter
2 tbsp golden syrup

90 ml/3 fl oz double cream
6 digestive biscuits,
    roughly crushed
50 g/2 oz shelled pistachio
    nuts, toasted and
    roughly chopped

50 g/2 oz blanched almonds,
    toasted and chopped
50 g/2 oz glacé cherries,
    roughly chopped
grated zest of 1 orange
cocoa powder, sifted

Lightly oil a 20.5 cm/8 inch square tin and line with clingfilm.

Place the sultanas into a small bowl and pour over the brandy, if using. Leave to soak for 20–30 minutes.

Meanwhile, break the chocolate into small pieces and put into a heatproof bowl. Place the bowl over a saucepan of simmering water, making sure that the bottom of the bowl does not touch the water.

Leave the chocolate until melted, stirring occasionally. Remove from the heat. Add the butter, golden syrup and double cream to a small saucepan and heat until the butter has melted.

Remove the saucepan from the heat and add the melted chocolate, biscuits, nuts, cherries, orange zest, sultanas and the brandy mixture.

Mix thoroughly and pour into the prepared tin. Smooth the top and chill in the refrigerator for at least 4 hours, or until firm.

Turn out the cake and remove the clingfilm. Dust liberally with the cocoa powder then cut into bars to serve. Store lightly covered in the refrigerator.

Try this: FOR AN ALTERNATIVE: 132   FOR A CAKE: 264

Fig & Chocolate Bars

MAKES 12

125 g/4 oz butter	brown sugar	juice of ½ a large lemon
150 g/5 oz plain flour	225 g/8 oz ready-to-eat	1 tsp ground cinnamon
50 g/2 oz soft light	dried figs, halved	125 g/4 oz plain dark chocolate

Preheat the oven to 180°C/350°F/Gas Mark 4, 10 minutes before baking. Lightly oil a 18 cm/7 inch square cake tin. Place the butter and the flour in a large bowl and, using your fingertips, rub the butter into the flour until it resembles fine breadcrumbs.

Stir in the sugar, then using your hands, bring the mixture together to form a smooth dough. Knead until smooth then press the dough into the prepared tin. Lightly prick the base with a fork and bake in the preheated oven for 20–30 minutes or until golden. Remove from the oven and leave the shortbread to cool in the tin until completely cold.

Meanwhile, place the dried figs, lemon juice, 125 ml/4 fl oz water and the ground cinnamon in a saucepan and bring to the boil. Cover and simmer for 20 minutes or until soft, stirring occasionally during cooking. Cool slightly, then purée in a food processor until smooth. Cool, then spread over the cooked shortbread.

Melt the chocolate in a heatproof bowl set over a saucepan of simmering water. Alternatively, the chocolate can be melted in the microwave, according to the manufacturer's instructions. Stir until smooth, then spread over the top of the fig filling. Leave to become firm, then cut into 12 bars and serve.

Try this: FOR AN ALTERNATIVE: 124 FOR A CAKE: 214

Apple & Cinnamon Crumble Bars

MAKES 16

450 g/1 lb Bramley cooking
   apples, roughly chopped
50 g/2 oz raisins
50 g/2 oz caster sugar
1 tsp ground cinnamon

zest of 1 lemon
200 g/7 oz plain flour
250 g/9 oz soft light
   brown sugar
½ tsp bicarbonate of soda

150 g/5 oz rolled oats
150 g/5 oz butter, melted
crème fraîche or whipped
   cream, to serve

Preheat the oven to 190˚C/375˚F/Gas Mark 5, 10 minutes before baking. Place the apples, raisins, sugar, cinnamon and lemon zest into a saucepan over a low heat.

Cover and cook for about 15 minutes, stirring occasionally, until the apple is cooked through. Remove the cover and stir well with a wooden spoon to break up the apple completely.

Cook for a further 15–30 minutes over a very low heat until reduced, thickened and slightly darkened. Allow to cool. Lightly oil and line a 20.5 cm/8 inch square cake tin with greaseproof or baking paper.

Mix together the flour, sugar, bicarbonate of soda, rolled oats and butter until combined well and crumbly. Spread half of the flour mixture into the bottom of the prepared tin and press down. Pour over the apple mixture.

Sprinkle over the remaining flour mixture and press down lightly. Bake in the preheated oven for 30–35 minutes, until golden brown.

Remove from the oven and allow to cool before cutting into slices. Serve the bars warm or cold with crème fraîche or whipped cream.

Try this: FOR AN ALTERNATIVE: 116   FOR A CAKE: 178

Apricot & Almond Slice

CUTS INTO 10 SLICES

2 tbsp demerara sugar
25 g/1 oz flaked almonds
400 g can apricot
 halves, drained
225 g/8 oz butter

225 g/8 oz caster sugar
4 medium eggs
200 g/7 oz self-raising flour
25 g/1 oz ground almonds
½ tsp almond essence

50 g/2 oz ready-to-eat dried
 apricots, chopped
3 tbsp clear honey
3 tbsp roughly chopped
 almonds, toasted

Preheat the oven to 180°C/350°F/Gas Mark 4. Oil a 20.5 cm/8 inch square tin and line with non-stick baking paper.

Sprinkle the sugar and the flaked almonds over the paper, then arrange the apricot halves cut-side down on top.

Cream the butter and sugar together in a large bowl until light and fluffy. Gradually beat the eggs into the butter mixture, adding a spoonful of flour after each addition of egg.

When all the eggs have been added, stir in the remaining flour and ground almonds and mix thoroughly. Add the almond essence and the apricots and stir well.

Spoon the mixture into the prepared tin, taking care not to dislodge the apricot halves. Bake in the preheated oven for 1 hour, or until golden and firm to touch.

Remove from the oven and allow to cool slightly for 15–20 minutes. Turn out carefully, discard the lining paper and transfer to a serving dish. Pour the honey over the top of the cake, sprinkle on the toasted almonds and serve.

Try this: FOR AN ALTERNATIVE: 104 FOR A CAKE: 224

Lemon Bars

MAKES 24

175 g/6 oz flour	2 tbsp flour	lightly beaten
125 g/4 oz butter	½ tsp baking powder	juice and finely grated
50 g/2 oz granulated sugar	¼ tsp salt	rind of 1 lemon
200 g/7 oz caster sugar	2 medium eggs,	sifted icing sugar, to decorate

Preheat the oven to 170°C/325°F/Gas Mark 3, 10 minutes before baking. Lightly oil and line a 20.5 cm/8 inch square cake tin with greaseproof or baking paper.

Rub together the flour and butter until the mixture resembles breadcrumbs. Stir in the granulated sugar and mix.

Turn the mixture into the prepared tin and press down firmly. Bake in the preheated oven for 20 minutes, until pale golden.

Meanwhile, in a food processor, mix together the caster sugar, flour, baking powder, salt, eggs, lemon juice and rind until smooth. Pour over the prepared base.

Transfer to the preheated oven and bake for a further 20–25 minutes, until nearly set but still a bit wobbly in the centre. Remove from the oven and cool in the tin on a wire rack.

Dust with icing sugar and cut into squares. Serve cold or store in an airtight tin.

Try this: FOR AN ALTERNATIVE: 108 FOR A CAKE: 188

Lemon–iced Ginger Squares

MAKES 12

225 g/8 oz caster sugar
50 g/2 oz butter, melted
2 tbsp black treacle
2 medium egg whites,
   lightly whisked

225 g/8 oz plain flour
1 tsp bicarbonate of soda
½ tsp ground cloves
1 tsp ground cinnamon
¼ tsp ground ginger

pinch of salt
225 ml/8 fl oz buttermilk
175 g/6 oz icing sugar
lemon juice

Preheat the oven to 200°C/400°F/Gas Mark 6, 15 minutes before baking. Lightly oil a
20.5 cm/8 inch square cake tin and sprinkle with a little flour.

Mix together the caster sugar, butter and treacle. Stir in the egg whites.

In a separate bowl, mix together the flour, bicarbonate of soda, cloves, cinnamon, ginger and
salt. Stir the flour mixture and buttermilk alternately into the butter mixture until blended well.

Spoon into the prepared tin and bake in the preheated oven for 35 minutes, or until a skewer
inserted into the centre of the cake comes out clean.

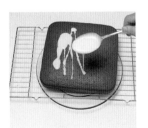

Remove from the oven and allow to cool for 5 minutes in the tin before turning out on to a wire
rack over a large plate. Using a cocktail stick, make holes on the top of the cake.

Meanwhile, mix together the icing sugar with enough lemon juice to make a smooth pourable
icing. Carefully pour the icing over the hot cake, then leave until cold. Cut the ginger cake into
squares and serve.

Try this: FOR AN ALTERNATIVE: 106   FOR A CAKE: 156

Fruit & Nut Flapjacks

MAKES 12

75 g/3 oz butter or margarine	3 tbsp golden syrup	175 g/6 oz rolled oats
125 g/4 oz soft light brown sugar	50 g/2 oz raisins	50 g/2 oz icing sugar
	50 g/2 oz walnuts, roughly chopped	1–1½ tbsp lemon juice

Preheat the oven to 180°C/350°F/Gas Mark 4, 10 minutes before baking. Lightly oil a 23 cm/9 inch square cake tin.

Melt the butter or margarine with the sugar and syrup in a small saucepan over a low heat. Remove from the heat. Stir the raisins, walnuts and oats into the syrup mixture and mix together well.

Spoon evenly into the prepared tin and press down well. Transfer to the preheated oven and bake for 20–25 minutes.

Remove from the oven and leave to cool in the tin. Cut into bars while still warm.

Sift the icing sugar into a small bowl then gradually beat in the lemon juice a little at a time to form a thin icing.

Place into an icing bag fitted with a writing nozzle then pipe thin lines over the flapjacks. Allow to cool and serve.

Try this: FOR AN ALTERNATIVE: 132   FOR A CAKE: 230

Chocolate–covered Flapjack

MAKES 24

215 g/7½ oz plain flour	1 tsp bicarbonate of soda	250 g/9 oz plain dark
150 g/5 oz rolled oats	pinch of salt	chocolate
225 g/8 oz light muscovado	150 g/5 oz butter	5 tbsp double cream
sugar	2 tbsp golden syrup	

Preheat the oven to 180°C/ 350°F/Gas Mark 4, 10 minutes before baking. Lightly oil a 33 x 23 cm/13 x 9 inch Swiss roll tin and line with nonstick baking parchment. Place the flour, rolled oats, the light muscovado sugar, bicarbonate of soda and salt into a bowl and stir well together.

Melt the butter and golden syrup together in a heavy-based saucepan and stir until smooth, then add to the oat mixture and mix together thoroughly. Spoon the mixture into the prepared tin and press down firmly and level the top.

Bake in the preheated oven for 15–20 minutes or until golden. Remove from the oven and leave the flapjack to cool in the tin. Once cool, remove from the tin. Discard the parchment.

Melt the chocolate in a heatproof bowl set over a saucepan of gently simmering water. Alternatively, melt the chocolate in the microwave according to the manufacturer's instructions. Once the chocolate has melted quickly beat in the cream, then pour over the flapjack. Mark patterns over the chocolate with a fork when almost set.

Chill the flapjack in the refrigerator for at least 30 minutes before cutting into bars. When the chocolate has set, serve. Store in an airtight container for a few days.

Try this: FOR AN ALTERNATIVE: 110 FOR A CAKE: 294

Chocolate Pecan Traybake

MAKES 12

175 g/6 oz butter
75 g/3 oz icing sugar, sifted
175 g/6 oz plain flour
25 g/1 oz self-raising flour
25 g/1 oz cocoa powder

For the pecan topping:
75 g/3 oz butter
50 g/2 oz light
   muscovado sugar
2 tbsp golden syrup

2 tbsp milk
1 tsp vanilla essence
2 medium eggs,
   lightly beaten
125 g/4 oz pecan halves

Preheat the oven to 180°C/350°F/Gas Mark 4, 10 minutes before baking. Lightly oil and line a 28 x 18 x 2.5 cm/11 x 7 x 1 inch cake tin with non-stick baking parchment.

Beat the butter and sugar together until light and fluffy. Sift in the flours and cocoa powder and mix together to form a soft dough.

Press the mixture evenly over the base of the prepared tin. Prick all over with a fork, then bake on the shelf above the centre of the preheated oven for 15 minutes.

Put the butter, sugar, golden syrup, milk and vanilla essence in a small saucepan and heat gently until melted. Remove from the heat and leave to cool for a few minutes, then stir in the eggs and pour over the base. Sprinkle with the nuts.

Bake in the preheated oven for 25 minutes or until dark golden brown, but still slightly soft. Leave to cool in the tin. When cool, carefully remove from the tin, then cut into 12 squares and serve. Store in an airtight container.

Try this: FOR AN ALTERNATIVE: 126 FOR A CAKE: 270

Fruit & Spice
Chocolate Slice

MAKES 10 SLICES

350 g/12 oz self-raising flour
1 tsp ground mixed spice
175 g/6 oz butter, chilled
125 g/4 oz plain
   dark chocolate,

roughly chopped
125 g/4 oz dried mixed fruit
75 g/3 oz dried apricots,
   chopped
75 g/3 oz chopped

mixed nuts
175 g/6 oz demerara sugar
2 medium eggs,
   lightly beaten
150 ml/¼ pint milk

Preheat the oven to 180°C/350°F/Gas Mark 4, 10 minutes before baking. Oil and line a deep 18 cm/7 inch square tin with nonstick baking parchment. Sift the flour and mixed spice into a large bowl. Cut the butter into small squares and, using your hands, rub in until the mixture resembles fine breadcrumbs.

Add the chocolate, dried mixed fruit, apricots and nuts to the dry ingredients. Reserve 1 tablespoon of the sugar, then add the rest to the bowl and stir. Add the eggs and half of the milk and mix together, then add enough of the remaining milk to give a soft dropping consistency.

Spoon the mixture into the prepared tin, level the surface with the back of a spoon and sprinkle with the reserved demerara sugar. Bake on the centre shelf of the preheated oven for 50 minutes. Cover the top with tinfoil to prevent the cake from browning too much and bake for a further 30–40 minutes, or until it is firm to the touch and a skewer inserted into the centre of the cake comes out clean.

Leave the cake in the tin for 10 minutes to cool slightly, then turn out onto a wire rack and leave to cool completely. Cut into 10 slices and serve. Store in an airtight container.

Try this: FOR AN ALTERNATIVE: 102 FOR A CAKE: 214

Chocolate Brazil & Polenta Squares

MAKES 9 SQUARES

150 g/5 oz shelled Brazil nuts	2 medium eggs, lightly beaten	1 tsp baking powder
150 g/5 oz butter, softened	75 g/3 oz plain flour	pinch of salt
150 g/5 oz soft light	25 g/1 oz cocoa powder	5 tbsp milk
brown sugar	¼ tsp ground cinnamon	60 g/2½ oz instant polenta

Preheat the oven to 180°C/350°F/Gas Mark 4, 10 minutes before baking. Oil and line a deep 18 cm/7 inch square tin with nonstick baking parchment. Finely chop 50 g/2 oz of the Brazil nuts and reserve. Roughly chop the remainder.

Cream the butter and sugar together until light and fluffy. Gradually add the eggs, beating well between each addition.

Sift the flour, cocoa powder, cinnamon, baking powder and salt into the creamed mixture and gently fold in using a large metal spoon or spatula.

Add the milk, polenta and the 75 g/3 oz of roughly chopped Brazil nuts. Fold into the mixture.

Turn the mixture into the prepared tin, levelling the surface with the back of the spoon. Sprinkle the reserved 50 g/2 oz of finely chopped Brazil nuts over the top. Bake the cake on the centre shelf of the preheated oven for 45–50 minutes, or until well risen and lightly browned and when a clean skewer inserted into the centre of the cake for a few seconds comes out clean.

Leave the cake in the tin for 10 minutes to cool slightly, then turn out onto a wire rack and leave to cool completely. Cut the cake into 9 equal squares and serve. Store in an airtight container.

Try this: FOR AN ALTERNATIVE: 120   FOR A CAKE: 170

Chocolate Walnut Squares

MAKES 24

125 g/4 oz butter
150 g/5 oz plain dark
  chocolate, broken
  into squares
450 g/1 lb caster sugar
½ tsp vanilla essence
200 g/7 oz plain flour

75 g/3 oz self-raising flour
50 g/2 oz cocoa powder
225 g/8 oz mayonnaise, at
  room temperature

For the chocolate glaze:
125 g/4 oz plain dark

chocolate, broken
  into squares
40 g/1½ oz unsalted butter
24 walnut halves
1 tbsp icing sugar,
  for dusting

Preheat the oven to 170°C/325°F/Gas Mark 3, 10 minutes before baking. Oil and line a 28 x 18 x 2.5 cm/11 x 7 x 1 inch cake tin with non-stick baking parchment.

Place the butter, chocolate, sugar, vanilla essence and 225 ml/8 fl oz of cold water in a heavy-based saucepan. Heat gently, stirring occasionally, until the chocolate and butter have melted, but do not allow to boil.

Sift the flours and cocoa powder into a large bowl and make a well in the centre. Add the mayonnaise and about one third of the chocolate mixture and beat until smooth. Gradually beat in the remaining chocolate mixture. Pour into the prepared tin and bake on the centre shelf of the preheated oven for 1 hour, or until slightly risen and firm to the touch. Place the tin on a wire rack and leave to cool. Remove the cake from the tin and peel off the parchment.

To make the chocolate glaze, place the chocolate and butter in a small saucepan with 1 tablespoon of water and heat very gently, stirring occasionally until melted and smooth. Leave to cool until the chocolate has thickened, then spread evenly over the cake. Chill the cake in the refrigerator for about 5 minutes, then mark into 24 squares. Lightly dust the walnut halves with a little icing sugar and place one on the top of each square. Cut into pieces and store in an airtight container until ready to serve.

Try this: FOR AN ALTERNATIVE: 118 FOR A CAKE: 262

Nanaimo Bars

MAKES 15

75 g/3 oz unsalted butter
125 g/4 oz plain
  dark chocolate,
  roughly chopped
75 g/3 oz digestive
  biscuits, crushed
75 g/3 oz desiccated coconut

50 g/2 oz chopped mixed nuts

For the filling:
1 medium egg yolk
1 tbsp milk
75 g/3 oz unsalted
  butter, softened

1 tsp vanilla essence
150 g/5 oz icing sugar

For the topping:
125 g/4 oz plain dark
  chocolate, chopped
2 tsp sunflower oil

Oil and line a 28 x 18 x 2.5 cm/11 x 7 x 1 inch cake tin with non-stick baking parchment.
Place the butter and chocolate in a heatproof bowl set over a saucepan of almost boiling water
until melted, stirring occasionally. Stir in the crushed biscuits, coconut and nuts into the
chocolate mixture and mix well. Spoon into the prepared tin and press down firmly. Chill in the
refrigerator for 20 minutes.

For the filling, place the egg yolk and milk in a heatproof bowl set over a saucepan of almost
boiling water, making sure the bowl does not touch the water. Whisk for 2–3 minutes. Add the
butter and vanilla essence to the bowl and continue whisking until fluffy, then gradually whisk
in the icing sugar. Spread over the chilled base, smoothing with the back of a spoon and chill
in the refrigerator for a further 30 minutes.

For the topping, place the chocolate and sunflower oil in a heatproof bowl set over a saucepan
of almost boiling water. Melt, stirring occasionally, until smooth. Leave to cool slightly, then
pour over the filling and tilt the tin, so that the chocolate spreads evenly.

Chill in the refrigerator for about 5 minutes, or until the chocolate topping is just set but not
too hard, then mark into 15 bars. Chill again in the refrigerator for 2 hours, then cut into slices
and serve.

Try this: FOR AN ALTERNATIVE: 126 FOR KIDS: 250

Miracle Bars

MAKES 12

100 g/3½ oz butter, melted,
plus 1–2 tsp extra
for oiling
125 g/4 oz digestive

biscuit crumbs
175 g/6 oz chocolate chips
75 g/3 oz shredded or
desiccated coconut

125 g/4 oz chopped
mixed nuts
400 g can sweetened
condensed milk

Preheat the oven to 180°C/350°F/Gas Mark 4, 10 minutes before baking. Generously butter a 23 cm/9 inch square tin and line with non-stick baking paper.

Pour the butter into the prepared tin and sprinkle the biscuit crumbs over in an even layer. Add the chocolate chips, coconut and nuts in even layers and drizzle over the condensed milk.

Transfer the tin to the preheated oven and bake for 30 minutes, until golden brown. Allow to cool in the tin, then cut into 12 squares and serve.

Try this: FOR AN ALTERNATIVE: 122   FOR A CAKE: 194

Pecan Caramel Millionaire's Shortbread

MAKES 20

125 g/4 oz butter, softened
2 tbsp smooth peanut butter
75 g/3 oz caster sugar
75 g/3 oz cornflour
175 g/6 oz plain flour

For the filling:
200 g/7 oz caster sugar
125 g/4 oz butter
2 tbsp golden syrup
75 g/3 oz liquid glucose
75 ml/3 fl oz water
400 g can sweetened

condensed milk
175 g/6 oz pecans,
  roughly chopped
For the topping:
75 g/3 oz plain dark
  chocolate
1 tbsp butter

Preheat the oven to 180°C/350°F/Gas Mark 4, 10 minutes before baking. Lightly oil and line an 18 cm x 28 cm/7 x 11 inch tin with greaseproof paper.

Cream together the butter, peanut butter and sugar until light. Sift in the cornflour and flour together and mix in to make a smooth dough. Press the mixture into the prepared tin and prick all over with a fork. Bake in the preheated oven for 20 minutes, until just golden. Remove from the oven.

Meanwhile, for the filling, combine the sugar, butter, golden syrup, glucose, water and milk in a heavy-based saucepan. Stir constantly over a low heat without boiling until the sugar has dissolved. Increase the heat and boil steadily, stirring constantly, for about 10 minutes until the mixture turns a golden caramel colour. Remove the saucepan from the heat and add the pecans. Pour over the shortbread base immediately. Allow to cool, then refrigerate for at least 1 hour.

Break the chocolate into small pieces and put into a heatproof bowl with the butter. Place over a saucepan of barely simmering water, ensuring that the bowl does not come into contact with the water. Leave until melted, then stir together well. Pour the chocolate evenly over the shortbread, spreading thinly to cover. Leave to set, cut into squares and serve.

Try this: FOR AN ALTERNATIVE: 100 FOR A CAKE: 270

Marbled Toffee Shortbread

MAKES 12

175 g/6 oz butter
75 g/3 oz caster sugar
175 g/6 oz plain flour
25 g/1 oz cocoa powder
75 g/3 oz fine semolina

For the toffee filling:
50 g/2 oz butter
50 g/2 oz soft light
 brown sugar

For the chocolate topping:
397 g can condensed milk
75 g/3 oz plain dark chocolate
75 g/3 oz milk chocolate
75 g/3 oz white chocolate

Preheat the oven to 180°C/350°F/Gas Mark 4, 10 minutes before baking. Oil and line a 20.5 cm /8 inch square cake tin with nonstick baking parchment. Cream the butter and sugar until light and fluffy then sift in the flour and cocoa powder. Add the semolina and mix together to form a soft dough. Press into the base of the prepared tin. Prick all over with a fork, then bake in the preheated oven for 25 minutes. Leave to cool.

To make the toffee filling, gently heat the butter, sugar and condensed milk together until the sugar has dissolved. Bring to the boil, then simmer for 5 minutes, stirring constantly. Leave for 1 minute, then spread over the shortbread and leave to cool.

For the topping, place the different chocolates in separate heatproof bowls and melt one at a time, set over a saucepan of almost boiling water. Drop spoonfuls of each on top of the toffee and tilt the tin to cover evenly. Swirl with a knife for a marbled effect.

Leave the chocolate to cool. When just set mark into fingers using a sharp knife. Leave for at least 1 hour to harden before cutting into fingers.

Try this: FOR AN ALTERNATIVE: 126 FOR A CAKE: 174

Indulgent
Chocolate Squares

MAKES 16

350 g/12 oz plain
  dark chocolate
175 g/6 oz butter, softened
175 g/6 oz soft light
  brown sugar
175 g/6 oz ground almonds

6 large eggs, separated
3 tbsp cocoa powder, sifted
75 g/3 oz fresh
  brown breadcrumbs
125 ml/4 fl oz double cream
50 g/2 oz white

chocolate, chopped
50 g/2 oz milk
  chocolate, chopped
few freshly sliced
  strawberries, to decorate

Preheat the oven to 180°C/350°F/Gas Mark 4, 10 minutes before baking. Oil and line a deep 20.5 cm/8 inch square cake tin with nonstick baking parchment. Melt 225 g/8 oz of the dark chocolate in a heatproof bowl set over a saucepan of almost boiling water. Stir until smooth, then leave until just cool, but not beginning to set.

Beat the butter and sugar until light and fluffy. Stir in the melted chocolate, ground almonds, egg yolks, cocoa powder and breadcrumbs.

Whisk the egg whites until stiff peaks form, then stir a large spoonful into the chocolate mixture. Gently fold in the rest, then pour the mixture into the prepared tin.

Bake on the centre shelf in the preheated oven for 1¼ hours, or until firm, covering the top with tinfoil after 45 minutes, to prevent it over-browning. Leave in the tin for 20 minutes, then turn out onto a wire rack and leave to cool.

Melt the remaining 125 g/4 oz plain chocolate with the cream in a heatproof bowl set over a saucepan of almost boiling water, stirring occasionally. Leave to cool for 20 minutes or until thickened slightly. Spread the topping over the cake. Scatter over the white and milk chocolate and leave to set. Cut into 16 squares and serve decorated with a few freshly sliced strawberries, then serve.

Try this: FOR AN ALTERNATIVE: 118   FOR A CAKE: 280

Fruit & Nut Refrigerator Fingers

MAKES 12

14 pink and white
    marshmallows
75 g/3 oz luxury dried mixed
    fruit
25 g/1 oz candied orange
    peel, chopped

75 g/3 oz glacé cherries,
    quartered
75 g/3 oz walnuts, chopped
1 tbsp brandy
175 g/6 oz digestive biscuits,
    crushed

225 g/8 oz plain dark
    chocolate
125 g/4 oz unsalted butter
1 tbsp icing sugar, for
    dusting, optional

Lightly oil and line the base of a 18 cm/7 inch tin with nonstick baking parchment. Using oiled kitchen scissors, snip each marshmallow into 4 or 5 pieces over a bowl. Add the dried mixed fruit, orange peel, cherries and walnuts to the bowl. Sprinkle with the brandy and stir together. Add the crushed biscuits and stir until mixed.

Break the chocolate into squares and put in a heatproof bowl with the butter set over a saucepan of almost boiling water. Stir occasionally until melted, then remove from the heat. Pour the melted chocolate mixture over the dry ingredients and mix together well. Spoon into the prepared tin, pressing down firmly.

Chill in the refrigerator for 15 minutes, then mark into 12 fingers using a sharp knife. Chill in the refrigerator for a further 1 hour or until set. Turn out of the tin, remove the lining paper and cut into fingers. Dust with icing sugar before serving.

Crunchy–topped Citrus Chocolate Slices

MAKES 12 SLICES

175 g/6 oz butter
175 g/6 oz soft light
  brown sugar
finely grated rind of 1 orange
3 medium eggs, lightly beaten
1 tbsp ground almonds

175 g/6 oz self-raising flour
¼ tsp baking powder
125 g/4 oz plain dark
  chocolate, coarsely grated
2 tsp milk

For the crunchy topping:
125 g/4 oz granulated sugar
juice of 2 limes
juice of 1 orange

Preheat the oven to 170°C/325°F/Gas Mark 3, 10 minutes before baking. Oil and line a 28 x 18 x 2.5 cm/11 x 7 x 1 inch cake tin with nonstick baking parchment. Place the butter, sugar and orange rind into a large bowl and cream together until light and fluffy. Gradually add the eggs, beating after each addition, then beat in the ground almonds.

Sift the flour and baking powder into the creamed mixture. Add the grated chocolate and milk, then gently fold in using a metal spoon. Spoon the mixture into the prepared tin.

Bake on the centre shelf of the preheated oven for 35–40 minutes, or until well risen and firm to the touch. Leave in the tin for a few minutes to cool slightly. Turn out onto a wire rack and remove the baking parchment.

Meanwhile, make the crunchy topping. Place the sugar with the lime and orange juices into a small jug and stir together. Drizzle the sugar mixture over the hot cake, ensuring the whole surface is covered. Leave until completely cold, then cut into 12 slices and serve.

Try this: FOR AN ALTERNATIVE: 108   FOR A CAKE: 186

All-in-one Chocolate Fudge Cakes

MAKES 15 SQUARES

175 g/6 oz soft dark
   brown sugar
175 g/6 oz butter, softened
150 g/5 oz self-raising flour
25 g/1 oz cocoa powder
1/2 tsp baking powder
pinch of salt

3 medium eggs,
   lightly beaten
1 tbsp golden syrup

For the fudge topping:
75 g/3 oz granulated sugar
150 ml/¼ pint evaporated milk

175 g/6 oz plain dark
   chocolate, roughly
   chopped
40 g/1½ oz unsalted
   butter, softened
125 g/4 oz soft fudge
   sweets, finely chopped

Preheat the oven to 180°C/350°F/Gas Mark 4, 10 minutes before baking. Oil and line a 28 x 18 x 2.5 cm/ 11 x 7 x 1 inch cake tin with non-stick baking parchment.

Place the soft brown sugar and butter in a bowl and sift in the flour, cocoa powder, baking powder and salt. Add the eggs and golden syrup, then beat with an electric whisk for 2 minutes, before adding 2 tablespoons of warm water and beating for a further 1 minute.

Turn the mixture into the prepared tin and level the top with the back of a spoon. Bake on the centre shelf of the preheated oven for 30 minutes, or until firm to the touch. Turn the cake out onto a wire rack and leave to cool before removing the baking parchment.

To make the topping, gently heat the sugar and evaporated milk in a saucepan, stirring frequently, until the sugar has dissolved. Bring the mixture to the boil and simmer for 6 minutes, without stirring.

Remove the mixture from the heat. Add the chocolate and butter and stir until melted and blended. Pour into a bowl and chill in the refrigerator for 1–2 hours or until thickened. Spread the topping over the cake, then sprinkle with the chopped fudge. Cut the cake into 15 squares before serving.

Try this: FOR AN ALTERNATIVE: 90 FOR A CAKE: 216

Marbled Chocolate Traybake

MAKES 18 SQUARES

175 g/6 oz butter
175 g/6 oz caster sugar
1 tsp vanilla essence
3 medium eggs,
    lightly beaten
200 g/7 oz self-raising flour

½ tsp baking powder
1 tbsp milk
1½ tbsp cocoa powder

For the chocolate icing:
75 g/3 oz plain dark

chocolate, broken
into pieces
75 g/3 oz white chocolate,
    broken into pieces

Preheat the oven to 180°C/350°F/Gas Mark 4, 10 minutes before baking. Oil and line a 28 x 18 x 2.5 cm/11 x 7 x 1 inch cake tin with non-stick baking parchment.

Cream the butter, sugar and vanilla essence until light and fluffy. Gradually add the eggs, beating well after each addition. Sift in the flour and baking powder and fold in with the milk.

Spoon half the mixture into the prepared tin, spacing the spoonfuls apart and leaving gaps in between. Blend the cocoa powder to a smooth paste with 2 tablespoons of warm water. Stir this into the remaining cake mixture. Drop small spoonfuls between the vanilla cake mixture to fill in all the gaps. Use a knife to swirl the mixtures together a little.

Bake on the centre shelf of the preheated oven for 35 minutes, or until well risen and firm to the touch. Leave in the tin for 5 minutes to cool, then turn out onto a wire rack and leave to cool. Remove the parchment.

For the icing, place the plain and white chocolate in separate heatproof bowls and melt each over a saucepan of almost boiling water. Spoon into separate non-stick baking parchment piping bags, snip off the tips and drizzle over the top. Leave to set before cutting into squares.

Light White Chocolate & Walnut Blondies

MAKES 15

75 g/3 oz unsalted butter
200 g/7 oz demerara sugar
2 large eggs, lightly beaten
1 tsp vanilla essence
2 tbsp milk

125 g/4 oz plain flour,
    plus 1 tbsp
1 tsp baking powder
pinch of salt
75 g/3 oz walnuts,

    roughly chopped
125 g/4 oz white
    chocolate drops
1 tbsp icing sugar

Preheat the oven to 190°C/375°F/Gas Mark 5, 10 minutes before baking. Oil and line a 28 x 18 x 2.5 cm/11 x 7 x 1 inch cake tin with non-stick baking parchment.

Place the butter and demerara sugar into a heavy-based saucepan and heat gently until the butter has melted and the sugar has started to dissolve. Remove from the heat and leave to cool.

Place the eggs, vanilla essence and milk in a large bowl and beat together. Stir in the butter and sugar mixture, then sift in the 125 g/4oz of flour, the baking powder and salt. Gently stir the mixture twice.

Toss the walnuts and chocolate drops in the remaining 1 tablespoon of flour to coat. Add to the bowl and stir the ingredients together gently.

Spoon the mixture into the prepared tin and bake on the centre shelf of the preheated oven for 35 minutes, or until the top is firm and slightly crusty. Place the tin on a wire rack and leave to cool. When completely cold, remove the cake from the tin and lightly dust the top with icing sugar. Cut into 15 blondies, using a sharp knife, and serve.

Small Cakes & Buns

Chunky Chocolate Muffins

MAKES 7

50 g/2 oz plain dark
chocolate, roughly
chopped
50 g/2 oz light
muscovado sugar
25 g/1 oz butter, melted

125 ml/4 fl oz milk, heated to
room temperature
½ tsp vanilla essence
1 medium egg, lightly beaten
150 g/5 oz self-raising flour
½ tsp baking powder

pinch of salt
75 g/3 oz white
chocolate, chopped
2 tsp icing sugar (optional)

Preheat the oven to 200°C/400°F/Gas Mark 6, 15 minutes before baking. Line a muffin or deep bun tin tray with seven paper muffin cases or oil the individual compartments well.

Place the plain chocolate in a large, heatproof bowl set over a saucepan of very hot water and stir occasionally until melted. Remove the bowl and leave to cool for a few minutes.

Stir the sugar and butter into the melted chocolate, then the milk, vanilla essence and egg. Sift in the flour, baking powder and salt together. Add the chopped white chocolate, then using a metal spoon, fold together quickly, taking care not to over mix.

Divide the mixture between the paper cases, piling it up in the centre. Bake on the centre shelf of the preheated oven for 20–25 minutes, or until well risen and firm to the touch.

Lightly dust the tops of the muffins with icing sugar as soon as they come out of the oven, if using. Leave the muffins in the tins for a few minutes, then transfer to a wire rack. Serve warm or cold.

Try this: FOR AN ALTERNATIVE: 146   FOR A COOKIE: 56

Fudgy & Top Hat Chocolate Buns

MAKES 12

50 g/2 oz self-raising flour
25 g/1 oz cocoa powder
½ tsp baking powder
75 g/3 oz butter, softened
75 g/3 oz soft light
  brown sugar
1 medium egg, lightly beaten
1 tbsp milk

For the fudgy icing:
15 g/½ oz unsalted
  butter, melted
1 tbsp milk
15 g/½ oz cocoa
  powder, sifted
40 g/1½ oz icing sugar, sifted
25 g/1 oz plain dark

For the top hat filling:
150 ml/¼ pint whipping
  cream
2 tsp orange liqueur
1 tbsp icing sugar, sifted
  chocolate, coarsely grated

Preheat the oven to 190°C/375°F/Gas Mark 5, 10 minutes before baking. Sift the flour, cocoa powder and baking powder into a bowl. Add the butter, sugar, egg and milk. Beat for 2–3 minutes or until light and fluffy.

Divide the mixture equally between 12 paper cases arranged in a bun tin tray. Bake on the shelf above the centre in the preheated oven for 15–20 minutes, or until well risen and firm to the touch. Leave in the bun tin for a few minutes, then transfer to a wire rack and leave to cool completely.

For the fudgy icing, mix together the melted butter, milk, cocoa powder and icing sugar. Place a spoonful of icing on the top of 6 of the buns, spreading out to a circle with the back of the spoon. Sprinkle with grated chocolate.

To make the top hats, use a sharp knife to cut and remove a circle of sponge, about 3 cm/1¼ inch across from each of the 6 remaining cakes. Whip the cream, orange liqueur and 1 teaspoon of icing sugar together until soft peaks form.

Spoon the filling into a piping bag fitted with a large star nozzle and pipe a swirl in the centre of each cake. Replace the tops, then dust with the remaining icing sugar and serve with the other buns.

Try this: FOR AN ALTERNATIVE: 136   FOR A COOKIE: 42

Chocolate & Orange Rock Buns

MAKES 12

200 g/7 oz self-raising flour
25 g/1 oz cocoa powder
½ tsp baking powder
125 g/4 oz butter
40 g/1½ oz granulated sugar
50 g/2 oz candied

pineapple, chopped
50 g/2 oz ready-to-eat dried
apricots, chopped
50 g/2 oz glacé cherries,
quartered
1 medium egg

finely grated rind of
½ orange
1 tbsp orange juice
2 tbsp demerara sugar

Preheat the oven to 200°C/400°F/Gas Mark 6, 15 minutes before baking. Lightly oil 2 baking sheets, or line them with nonstick baking parchment. Sift the flour, cocoa powder and baking powder into a bowl. Cut the butter into small squares. Add to the dry ingredients, then, using your hands, rub in until the mixture resembles fine breadcrumbs.

Add the granulated sugar, pineapple, apricots and cherries to the bowl and stir to mix. Lightly beat the egg together with the grated orange rind and juice. Drizzle the egg mixture over the dry ingredients and stir to combine. The mixture should be fairly stiff but not too dry, add a little more orange juice, if needed.

Using 2 teaspoons, shape the mixture into 12 rough heaps on the prepared baking sheets. Sprinkle generously with the demerara sugar. Bake in the preheated oven for 15 minutes, switching the baking sheets around after 10 minutes. Leave on the baking sheets for 5 minutes to cool slightly, then transfer to a wire rack to cool. Serve warm or cold.

Try this: FOR AN ALTERNATIVE: 156   FOR A COOKIE: 82

Rich Chocolate Cup Cakes

MAKES 12

175 g/6 oz self-raising flour
25 g/1 oz cocoa powder
175 g/6 oz soft light
   brown sugar
75 g/3 oz butter, melted
2 medium eggs,
   lightly beaten
1 tsp vanilla essence

40 g/1½ oz maraschino
   cherries, drained
   and chopped

For the chocolate icing:
50 g/2 oz plain
   dark chocolate
25 g/1 oz unsalted butter

25 g/1 oz icing sugar, sifted
For the cherry icing:
125 g/4 oz icing sugar
7 g/¼ oz unsalted butter, melted
1 tsp syrup from the
   maraschino cherries
3 maraschino cherries,
   halved, to decorate

Preheat the oven to 180°C/350°F/Gas Mark 4, 10 minutes before baking. Line a 12 hole muffin or deep bun tin tray with paper muffin cases.

Sift the flour and cocoa powder into a bowl. Stir in the sugar, then add the melted butter, eggs and vanilla essence. Beat together with a wooden spoon for 3 minutes or until well blended. Divide half the mixture between six of the paper cases. Dry the cherries thoroughly on absorbent kitchen paper, then fold into the remaining mixture and spoon into the rest of the paper cases. Bake on the shelf above the centre of the preheated oven for 20 minutes, or until a skewer inserted into the centre of a cake comes out clean. Transfer to a wire rack and leave to cool.

For the chocolate icing, melt the chocolate and butter in a heatproof bowl set over a saucepan of hot water. Remove from the heat and leave to cool for 3 minutes, stirring occasionally. Stir in the icing sugar. Spoon over the six plain chocolate cakes and leave to set.

For the cherry icing, sift the icing sugar into a bowl and stir in 1 tablespoon of boiling water, the butter and cherry syrup. Spoon the icing over the remaining six cakes, decorate each with a halved cherry and leave to set.

Try this: FOR AN ALTERNATIVE: 146 FOR A COOKIE: 84

Cappuccino Cakes

MAKES 6

125 g/4 oz butter or margarine
125 g/4 oz caster sugar
2 medium eggs

1 tbsp strong black coffee
150 g/5 oz self-raising flour
125 g/4 oz mascarpone cheese

1 tbsp icing sugar, sifted
1 tsp vanilla essence
sifted cocoa powder, to dust

Preheat the oven to 190°C/375°F/Gas Mark 5, 10 minutes before baking. Place six large paper muffin cases into a muffin tin or alternatively place on to a baking sheet.

Cream the butter or margarine and sugar together until light and fluffy. Break the eggs into a small bowl and beat lightly with a fork. Using a wooden spoon, beat the eggs into the butter and sugar mixture a little at a time, until they are all incorporated.

If the mixture looks curdled beat in a spoonful of the flour to return the mixture to a smooth consistency. Finally beat in the black coffee.

Sift the flour into the mixture, then with a metal spoon or rubber spatula gently fold in the flour. Place spoonfuls of the mixture into the muffin cases.

Bake in the preheated oven for 20–25 minutes, or until risen and springy to the touch. Cool on a wire rack.

In a small bowl beat together the mascarpone cheese, icing sugar and vanilla essence. When the cakes are cold, spoon the vanilla mascarpone on to the top of each one. Dust with cocoa powder and serve. Eat within 24 hours and store in the refrigerator.

Try this: FOR AN ALTERNATIVE: 150   FOR A COOKIE: 30

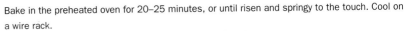

Chocolate Madeleines

MAKES 10

125 g/4 oz butter
125 g/4 oz soft light
   brown sugar
2 medium eggs,
   lightly beaten
1 drop almond essence
1 tbsp ground almonds

75 g/3 oz self-raising flour
20 g/¾ oz cocoa powder
1 tsp baking powder

To finish:
5 tbsp apricot conserve
1 tbsp amaretto liqueur,

brandy or orange juice
50 g/2 oz desiccated coconut
10 large chocolate buttons
   (optional)

Preheat the oven to 180°C/350°F/Gas Mark 4, 10 minutes before baking. Lightly oil 10 dariole moulds and line the bases of each with a small circle of non-stick baking parchment. Stand the moulds on a baking tray.

Cream the butter and sugar together until light and fluffy. Gradually add the eggs, beating well between each addition. Beat in the almond essence and ground almonds.

Sift the flour, cocoa powder and baking powder over the creamed mixture. Gently fold in using a metal spoon. Divide the mixture equally between the prepared moulds – each should be about half full.

Bake on the centre shelf of the preheated oven for 20 minutes, or until well risen and firm to the touch. Leave in the tins for a few minutes, then run a small palette knife round the edge and turn out onto a wire rack to cool. Remove the paper circles from the sponges.

Heat the conserve with the liqueur, brandy or juice in a small saucepan. Sieve to remove any lumps. If necessary, trim the sponge bases, so they are flat. Brush the tops and sides with warm conserve, then roll in the coconut. Top each with a chocolate button, fixed by brushing its base with conserve.

Try this: FOR AN ALTERNATIVE: 144   FOR A COOKIE: 58

Lemon & Ginger Buns

MAKES 15

175 g/6 oz butter or margarine
350 g/12 oz plain flour
2 tsp baking powder
½ tsp ground ginger
pinch of salt

finely grated rind of 1 lemon
175 g/6 oz soft light
    brown sugar
125 g/4 oz sultanas
75 g/3 oz chopped mixed peel

25 g/1 oz stem ginger,
    finely chopped
1 medium egg
juice of 1 lemon

Preheat the oven to 220°C/425°F/Gas Mark 7, 15 minutes before baking. Cut the butter or margarine into small pieces and place in a large bowl. Sift the flour, baking powder, ginger and salt together and add to the butter with the lemon rind.

Using the fingertips rub the butter into the flour and spice mixture until it resembles coarse breadcrumbs. Stir in the sugar, sultanas, chopped mixed peel and stem ginger.

Add the egg and lemon juice to the mixture, then using a round bladed knife stir well to mix. (The mixture should be quite stiff and just holding together.)

Place heaped tablespoons of the mixture on to a lightly oiled baking tray, making sure that the dollops of mixture are well apart. Using a fork rough up the edges of the buns and bake in the preheated oven for 12–15 minutes.

Leave the buns to cool for 5 minutes before transferring to a wire rack until cold, then serve. Otherwise store the buns in an airtight tin and eat within 3–5 days.

Try this: FOR AN ALTERNATIVE: 156   FOR A COOKIE: 62

Spiced Apple Doughnuts

MAKES 8

225 g/8 oz strong white flour
½ tsp salt
1½ tsp ground cinnamon
1 tsp easy-blend dried yeast
75 ml/3 fl oz warm milk

25 g/1 oz butter, melted
1 medium egg, beaten
oil, to deep-fry
4 tbsp caster sugar, to coat

For the filling:
2 small eating apples, peeled, cored and chopped
2 tsp soft light brown sugar
2 tsp lemon juice

Sift the flour, salt and 1 teaspoon of the cinnamon into a large bowl. Stir in the yeast and make a well in the centre. Add the milk, butter and egg and mix to a soft dough. Knead on a lightly floured surface for 10 minutes, until smooth and elastic.

Divide the dough into 8 pieces and shape each into a ball. Put on a floured baking sheet, cover with oiled clingfilm and leave in a warm place for 1 hour, or until doubled in size.

To make the filling, put the apples in a saucepan with the sugar, lemon juice and 3 tablespoons of water. Cover and simmer for about 10 minutes, then uncover and cook until fairly dry, stirring occasionally. Mash or blend in a food processor to a purée.

Pour enough oil into a deep-fat frying pan to come one-third of the way up the pan. Heat the oil to 180°C/350°F, then deep-fry the doughnuts for 1½–2 minutes on each side, until well browned.

Drain the doughnuts on kitchen paper, then roll in the caster sugar mixed with the remaining ½ teaspoon of ground cinnamon. Push a thick skewer into the centre to make a hole, then pipe in the apple filling. Serve warm or cold.

Try this: FOR AN ALTERNATIVE: 1254   FOR A COOKIE: 52

Jammy Buns

MAKES 12

175 g/6 oz plain flour
175 g/6 oz wholemeal flour
2 tsp baking powder
150 g/5 oz butter

or margarine
125 g/4 oz golden
    caster sugar
50 g/2 oz dried cranberries

1 large egg, beaten
1 tbsp milk
4–5 tbsp seedless
    raspberry jam

Preheat the oven to 190°C/375°F/Gas Mark 5, 10 minutes before baking. Lightly oil a large baking sheet.

Sift the flours and baking powder together into a large bowl, then tip in the grains remaining in the sieve.

Cut the butter or margarine into small pieces. It is easier to do this when the butter is in the flour as it helps stop the butter from sticking to the knife.

Rub the butter into the flours until it resembles coarse breadcrumbs. Stir in the sugar and cranberries.

Using a round bladed knife stir in the beaten egg and milk. Mix to form a firm dough. Divide the mixture into 12 and roll into balls.

Place the dough balls on the baking tray, leaving enough space for expansion. Press your thumb into the centre of each ball to make a small hollow. Spoon a little of the jam in each hollow. Pinch lightly to seal the tops.

Bake in the preheated oven for 20–25 minutes, or until golden brown. Cool on a wire rack and serve.

Try this: FOR AN ALTERNATIVE: 158 FOR A COOKIE: 86

Fruited Brioche Buns

MAKES 12

225 g/8 oz strong white flour
pinch of salt
1 tbsp caster sugar
7 g/¼ oz sachet easy-blend
   dried yeast
2 large eggs, beaten

50 g/2 oz butter, melted
beaten egg, to glaze

For the filling:
40 g/1½ oz blanched
   almonds, chopped

50 g/2 oz luxury mixed
   dried fruit
1 tsp light soft brown sugar
2 tsp orange liqueur or
   brandy

Preheat the oven to 220°C/425°F/Gas Mark 7, 15 minutes before baking. Sift the flour and salt into a bowl. Stir in the sugar and yeast. Make a well in the centre. Add the eggs, butter and 2 tablespoons of warm water and mix to a soft dough.

Knead the dough on a floured surface for 5 minutes, until smooth and elastic. Put in an oiled bowl, cover with clingfilm and leave to rise in a warm place for 1 hour, or until it has doubled in size.

Mix the filling ingredients together, cover the bowl and leave to soak while the dough is rising.

Re-knead the dough for a minute or two, then divide into 12 pieces. Take 1 piece at a time and flatten three-quarters into a 6.5 cm/2½ inch round. Spoon a little filling in the centre, then pinch the edges together to enclose. Put seam-side down into a well-greased fluted 12-hole bun tin.

Shape the smaller piece of dough into a round and place on top of the larger one. Push a finger or floured wooden spoon handle through the middle of the top one and into the bottom one to join them together. Repeat with the remaining balls of dough. Cover the brioche with oiled clingfilm and leave for about 20 minutes, or until well risen.

Brush the brioches with beaten egg and bake in the preheated oven for 10–12 minutes, or until golden. Cool on a wire rack and serve.

Try this: FOR AN ALTERNATIVE: 164   FOR A COOKIE: 46

Chocolate Chelsea Buns

MAKES 12

75 g/3 oz dried pears,
   finely chopped
1 tbsp apple or orange juice
225 g/8 oz strong plain flour
1 tsp ground cinnamon

½ tsp salt
40 g/1½ oz butter
1½ tsp easy-blend
   dried yeast
125 ml/4 fl oz warm milk

1 medium egg,
   lightly beaten
75 g/3 oz plain dark
   chocolate, chopped
3 tbsp maple syrup

Preheat the oven to 190°C/375°F/Gas Mark 5, 10 minutes before baking. Lightly oil an 18 cm /7 inch square tin. Place the pears in a bowl with the fruit juice, stir then cover and leave to soak while making the dough.

Sift the flour, cinnamon and salt into a bowl, rub in 25 g/1 oz of the butter then stir in the yeast and make a well in the middle. Add the milk and egg and mix to a soft dough. Knead on a floured surface for 10 minutes, until smooth and elastic, then place in a bowl. Cover with clingfilm and leave in a warm place to rise for 1 hour or until doubled in size.

Turn out on a lightly floured surface and knead the dough lightly before rolling out to a rectangle, about 30.5 x 23 cm/12 x 9 inches. Melt the remaining butter and brush over. Spoon the pears and chocolate evenly over the dough leaving a 2.5 cm/1 inch border, then roll up tightly, starting at a long edge. Cut into 12 equal slices, then place, cut-side up in the tin. Cover and leave to rise for 25 minutes, or until doubled in size.

Bake on the centre shelf of the preheated oven for 30 minutes, or until well risen and golden brown. Cover with tinfoil after 20 minutes, if the filling is starting to brown too much.

Brush with the maple syrup while hot, then leave in the tin for 10 minutes to cool slightly. Turn out onto a wire rack and leave to cool. Separate the buns and serve warm.

Try this: FOR AN ALTERNATIVE: 162   FOR A COOKIE: 36

Everyday Cakes

Moist Mincemeat Tea Loaf

CUTS INTO 12 SLICES

225 g/8 oz self-raising flour
½ tsp ground mixed spice
125 g/4 oz cold butter, cubed
75 g/3 oz flaked almonds
25 g/1 oz glacé cherries,

rinsed, dried
and quartered
75 g/3 oz light
muscovado sugar
2 medium eggs

250 g/9 oz prepared
mincemeat
1 tsp lemon zest
2 tsp brandy or milk

Preheat the oven to 180°C/350°F/Gas Mark 4, 10 minutes before cooking. Oil and line the base of a 900 g/2 lb loaf tin with non-stick baking paper.

Sift the flour and mixed spice into a large bowl. Add the butter and rub in until the mixture resembles breadcrumbs.

Reserve 2 tablespoons of the flaked almonds and stir in the rest with the glacé cherries and sugar. Make a well in the centre of the dry ingredients. Lightly whisk the eggs, then stir in the mincemeat, lemon zest and brandy or milk.

Add the egg mixture and fold together until blended. Spoon into the prepared loaf tin, smooth the top with the back of a spoon, then sprinkle over the reserved flaked almonds.

Bake on the middle shelf of the preheated oven for 30 minutes. Cover with tinfoil to prevent the almonds browning too much. Bake for a further 30 minutes, or until well risen and a skewer inserted into the centre comes out clean.

Leave the tea loaf in the tin for 10 minutes before removing and cooling on a wire rack. Remove the lining paper, slice thickly and serve.

Try this: FOR AN ALTERNATIVE: 176 FOR A COOKIE OR TRAYBAKE: 46

Maple, Pecan & Lemon Loaf

CUTS TO 12 SLICES

350 g/12 oz plain flour
1 tsp baking powder
175 g/6 oz butter, cubed
75 g/3 oz caster sugar
125 g/4 oz pecan nuts,

roughly chopped
3 medium eggs
1 tbsp milk
finely grated rind of 1 lemon
5 tbsp maple syrup

For the icing:
75 g/3 oz icing sugar
1 tbsp lemon juice
25 g/1 oz pecans,
roughly chopped

Preheat the oven to 170°C/325°F/Gas Mark 3, 10 minutes before baking. Lightly oil and line the base of a 900 g/2 lb loaf tin with non-stick baking parchment.

Sift the flour and baking powder into a large bowl. Rub in the butter until the mixture resembles fine breadcrumbs. Stir in the caster sugar and pecan nuts.

Beat the eggs together with the milk and lemon rind. Stir in the maple syrup. Add to the dry ingredients and gently stir in until mixed thoroughly to make a soft dropping consistency.

Spoon the mixture into the prepared tin and level the top with the back of a spoon. Bake on the middle shelf of the preheated oven for 50–60 minutes, or until the cake is well risen and lightly browned. If a skewer inserted into the centre comes out clean, then the cake is ready.

Leave the cake in the tin for about 10 minutes, then turn out and leave to cool on a wire rack. Carefully remove the lining paper.

Sift the icing sugar into a small bowl and stir in the lemon juice to make a smooth icing.

Drizzle the icing over the top of the loaf, then scatter with the chopped pecans. Leave to set, thickly slice and serve.

Try this: FOR AN ALTERNATIVE: 188 FOR A COOKIE OR TRAYBAKE: 42

Marbled Chocolate & Orange Loaf

CUTS INTO 6 SLICES

50 g/2 oz plain dark
chocolate, broken
into squares
125 g/4 oz butter, softened
125 g/4 oz caster sugar

zest of 1 orange
2 medium eggs, beaten
125 g/4 oz self-raising flour
2 tsp orange juice
1 tbsp cocoa powder, sifted

To finish:
1 tbsp icing sugar
1 tsp cocoa powder

Preheat the oven to 180°C/350°F/Gas Mark 4. Lightly oil a 450 g/1 lb loaf tin and line the base with a layer of non-stick baking paper.

Put the chocolate in a bowl over a saucepan of very hot water. Stir occasionally until melted. Remove and leave until just cool, but not starting to reset.

Meanwhile, cream together the butter, sugar and orange zest until pale and fluffy. Gradually add the beaten eggs, beating well after each addition. Sift in the flour, add the orange juice and fold with a metal spoon or rubber spatula. Divide the mixture by half into two separate bowls. Gently fold the cocoa powder and chocolate into one half of the mixture.

Drop tablespoonfuls of each cake mixture into the prepared tin, alternating between the orange and chocolate mixtures. Briefly swirl the colours together with a knife to give a marbled effect.

Bake in the preheated oven for 40 minutes, or until firm and a fine skewer inserted into the centre comes out clean. Leave in the tin for 5 minutes, then turn out and cool on a wire rack. Carefully remove the lining paper.

Dust the cake with the icing sugar and then with the cocoa powder. Cut into thick slices and serve.

Try this: FOR AN ALTERNATIVE: 174 FOR A COOKIE OR TRAYBAKE: 82

Marble Cake

CUTS INTO 8 SLICES

225 g/8 oz butter or margarine
225 g/8 oz caster sugar
4 medium eggs
225 g/8 oz self-raising

flour, sifted
finely grated rind and
juice of 1 orange
25 g/1 oz cocoa powder, sifted

For the topping:
zest and juice of 1 orange
1 tbsp granulated sugar

Preheat the oven to 190°C/375°F/Gas Mark 5, 10 minutes before baking. Lightly oil and line the base of an 20.5 cm/8 inch deep round cake tin with greaseproof or baking paper.

In a large bowl, cream the butter or margarine and sugar together until light and fluffy. Beat the eggs together. Beat into the creamed mixture a little at a time, beating well between each addition. When all the egg has been added, fold in the flour with a metal spoon or rubber spatula.

Divide the mixture equally between 2 bowls. Beat the grated orange rind into one of the bowls with a little of the orange juice. Mix the cocoa powder with the remaining orange juice until smooth, then add to the other bowl and beat well.

Spoon the mixture into the prepared tin, in alternate spoonfuls. When all the cake mixture is in the tin, take a skewer and swirl it in the 2 mixtures. Tap the base of the tin on the work surface to level the mixture. Bake in the preheated oven for 50 minutes, or until cooked and a skewer inserted into the centre of the cake comes out clean. Remove from the oven and leave in the tin for a few minutes before cooling on a wire rack. Discard the lining paper.

For the topping, place the orange zest and juice with the granulated sugar in a small saucepan and heat gently until the sugar has dissolved. Bring to the boil and simmer gently for 3–4 minutes, until the juice is syrupy. Pour over the cooled cake and serve when cool. Otherwise, store in an airtight tin.

Try this: FOR AN ALTERNATIVE: 172 FOR A COOKIE OR TRAYBAKE: 76

Fruity Apple Tea Bread

CUTS INTO 12 SLICES

125 g/4 oz butter
125 g/4 oz soft light
brown sugar
275 g/10 oz sultanas
150 ml/¼ pint apple juice
1 eating apple, peeled cored
and chopped

2 medium eggs, beaten
275 g/10 oz plain flour
½ tsp ground cinnamon
½ tsp ground ginger

To decorate:
1 eating apple, cored
and sliced
2 tsp bicarbonate of soda
curls of butter, to serve
1 tsp lemon juice
1 tbsp golden syrup, warmed

Preheat the oven to 180°C/350°F/Gas Mark 4. Oil and line the base of a 900 g/2 lb loaf tin with non-stick baking paper.

Put the butter, sugar, sultanas and apple juice in a small saucepan. Heat gently, stirring occasionally until the butter has melted. Tip into a bowl and leave to cool. Stir in the chopped apple and beaten eggs. Sift the flour, spices and bicarbonate of soda over the apple mixture. Stir into the sultana mixture, spoon into the prepared loaf tin and smooth the top level with the back of a spoon.

Toss the apple slices in lemon juice and arrange on top. Bake in the preheated oven for 50 minutes. Cover with tinfoil to prevent the top from browning too much.

Bake for 30–35 minutes, or until a skewer inserted into the centre comes out clean.

Leave in the tin for 10 minutes before turning out to cool on to a wire rack. Brush the top with golden syrup and leave to cool. Remove the lining paper, cut into thick slices and serve with curls of butter.

Try this: FOR AN ALTERNATIVE: 178   FOR A COOKIE OR TRAYBAKE: 52

Apple & Cinnamon Crumble–top Cake

CUTS INTO 8 SLICES

For the topping:
350 g/12 oz eating
   apples, peeled
1 tbsp lemon juice
125 g/4 oz self-raising flour
1 tsp ground cinnamon
75 g/3 oz butter or margarine

75 g/3 oz demerara sugar
1 tbsp milk

For the base:
125 g/4 oz butter or margarine
125 g/4 oz caster sugar
2 medium eggs

150 g/5 oz self-raising flour

cream or freshly made
   custard, to serve.

Preheat the oven to 180°C/350°F/Gas Mark 4, 10 minutes before baking. Lightly oil and line the base of a 20.5 cm/8 inch deep round cake tin with greaseproof or baking paper.

Finely chop the apples and mix with the lemon juice. Reserve while making the cake.

For the crumble topping, sift the flour and cinnamon together into a large bowl. Rub the butter or margarine into the flour and cinnamon until the mixture resembles coarse breadcrumbs. Stir the sugar into the mixture and reserve.

For the base, cream the butter or margarine and sugar together until light and fluffy. Gradually beat the eggs into the sugar and butter mixture a little at a time until all the egg has been added. Sift the flour and gently fold in with a metal spoon or rubber spatula.

Spoon into the base of the prepared cake tin. Arrange the apple pieces on top, then lightly stir the milk into the crumble mixture.

Scatter the crumble mixture over the apples and bake in the preheated oven for 1½ hours. Serve cold with cream or custard.

Try this: FOR AN ALTERNATIVE: 228   FOR A COOKIE OR TRAYBAKE: 50

Toffee Apple Cake

CUTS INTO 8 SLICES

2 small eating apples, peeled
4 tbsp soft dark brown sugar
175 g/6 oz butter or margarine
175 g/6 oz caster sugar

3 medium eggs
175 g/6 oz self-raising flour
150 ml/¼ pint double cream
2 tbsp icing sugar

½ tsp vanilla essence
½ tsp ground cinnamon

Preheat the oven to 180°C/350°F/Gas Mark 4, 10 minutes before baking time. Lightly oil and line the bases of 2 x 20.5 cm/8 inch sandwich tins with greaseproof or baking paper.

Thinly slice the apples and toss in the brown sugar until well coated. Arrange them over the base of the prepared tins and reserve.

Cream together the butter or margarine and caster sugar until light and fluffy.

Beat the eggs together in a small bowl and gradually beat them into the creamed mixture, beating well between each addition.

Sift the flour into the mixture and using a metal spoon or rubber spatula, fold in. Divide the mixture between the 2 cake tins and level the surface.

Bake in the preheated oven for 25–30 minutes, until golden and well risen. Leave in the tins to cool.

Lightly whip the cream with 1 tablespoon of the icing sugar and vanilla essence. Sandwich the cakes together with the cream. Mix the remaining icing sugar and ground cinnamon together, sprinkle over the top of the cake and serve.

Try this: FOR AN ALTERNATIVE: 176   FOR A COOKIE OR TRAYBAKE: 68

Fruit Cake

CUTS INTO 10 SLICES

225 g/8 oz butter or margarine
200 g/7 oz soft brown sugar
finely grated rind of 1 orange
1 tbsp black treacle
3 large eggs, beaten
275 g/10 oz plain flour

¼ tsp ground cinnamon
½ tsp mixed spice
pinch of freshly
  grated nutmeg
¼ tsp bicarbonate of soda
75 g/3 oz mixed peel

50 g/2 oz glacé cherries
125 g/4 oz raisins
125 g/4 oz sultanas
125 g/4 oz ready-to-eat dried
  apricots, chopped

Preheat the oven to 150°C/300°C/Gas Mark 2, 10 minutes before baking. Lightly oil and line a deep 23 cm/9 inch round cake tin with a double thickness of greaseproof paper.

In a large bowl cream together the butter or margarine, sugar and orange rind, until light and fluffy, then beat in the treacle. Beat in the eggs a little at a time, beating well between each addition.

Reserve 1 tablespoon of the flour. Sift the remaining flour, the spices and bicarbonate of soda into the mixture. Mix all the fruits and the reserved flour together, then stir into the cake mixture.

Turn into the prepared tin and smooth the top, making a small hollow in the centre of the cake mixture.

Bake in the preheated oven for 1 hour, then reduce the heat to 140°C/275°F/Gas Mark 1.

Bake for a further 1½ hours, or until cooked and a skewer inserted into the centre comes out clean. Leave to cool in the tin, then turn the cake out and serve. Otherwise, when cold store in an airtight tin.

Try this: FOR AN ALTERNATIVE: 230 FOR A COOKIE OR TRAYBAKE: 46

Banana Cake

CUTS INTO 8 SLICES

3 medium-sized ripe bananas
1 tsp lemon juice
150 g/5 oz soft brown sugar
75 g/3 oz butter
   or margarine

250 g/9 oz self-raising flour
1 tsp ground cinnamon
3 medium eggs
50 g/2 oz walnuts, chopped
1 tsp each ground cinnamon

and caster sugar,
   to decorate
fresh cream, to serve

Preheat the oven to 190°C/375°F/Gas Mark 5, 10 minutes before baking. Lightly oil and line the base of a deep 18 cm/7 inch round cake tin with greaseproof or baking paper.

Mash two of the bananas in a small bowl, sprinkle with the lemon juice and a heaped tablespoon of the sugar. Mix together lightly and reserve.

Gently heat the remaining sugar and butter or margarine in a small saucepan until the butter has just melted. Pour into a small bowl, then allow to cool slightly. Sift the flour and cinnamon into a large bowl and make a well in the centre.

Beat the eggs into the cooled sugar mixture, pour into the well of flour, and mix thoroughly. Gently stir in the mashed banana mixture. Pour half of the mixture into the prepared tin. Thinly slice the remaining banana and arrange over the cake mixture. Sprinkle over the chopped walnuts, then cover with the remaining cake mixture.

Bake in the preheated oven for 50–55 minutes, or until well risen and golden brown. Allow to cool in the tin, turn out and sprinkle with the ground cinnamon and caster sugar. Serve hot or cold with a jug of fresh cream for pouring.

Try this: FOR AN ALTERNATIVE: 190 FOR A COOKIE OR TRAYBAKE: 60

Citrus Cake

CUTS INTO 8 SLICES

175 g/6 oz golden caster sugar
175 g/6 oz butter or margarine
3 medium eggs

2 tbsp orange juice
175 g/6 oz self-raising flour
finely grated rind of 2 oranges
5 tbsp lemon curd

125 g/4 oz icing sugar
finely grated rind of 1 lemon
1 tbsp freshly squeezed lemon juice

Preheat the oven to 325°C/170°F/Gas Mark 3, 10 minutes before baking. Lightly oil and line the base of a deep, round 20.5 cm/8 inch cake tin with baking paper.

In a large bowl, cream the sugar and butter or margarine together until light and fluffy. Whisk the eggs together and beat into the creamed mixture a little at a time.

Beat in the orange juice with 1 tablespoon of the flour. Sift the remaining flour on to a large plate several times, then with a metal spoon or rubber spatula, fold into the creamed mixture.

Spoon into the prepared cake tin. Stir the finely grated orange rind into the lemon curd and dot randomly across the top of the mixture.

Using a fine skewer swirl the lemon curd through the cake mixture. Bake in the preheated oven for 35 minutes, until risen and golden. Allow to cool for 5 minutes in the tin, then turn out carefully on to a wire rack.

Sift the icing sugar into a bowl, add the grated lemon rind and juice and stir well to mix. When the cake is cold, cover the top with the icing and serve.

Try this: FOR AN ALTERNATIVE: 248   FOR A COOKIE OR TRAYBAKE: 134

Lemon Drizzle Cake

CUTS INTO 16 SQUARES

125 g/4 oz butter or
   margarine
175 g/6 oz caster sugar

2 large eggs
175 g/6 oz self-raising flour
2 lemons, preferably

unwaxed
50 g/2 oz granulated
   sugar

Preheat the oven to 180°C/350°F/Gas Mark 4, 10 minutes before baking. Lightly oil and line the base of an 18 cm/7 inch square cake tin with baking paper.

In a large bowl, cream the butter or margarine and sugar together until soft and fluffy. Beat the eggs, then gradually add a little of the egg to the creamed mixture, adding 1 tablespoon of flour after each addition.

Finely grate the rind from 1 of the lemons and stir into the creamed mixture, beating well until smooth. Squeeze the juice from the lemon, strain, then stir into the mixture.

Spoon into the prepared tin, level the surface and bake in the preheated oven for 25–30 minutes. Using a zester, remove the peel from the last lemon and mix with 25 g/1 oz of the granulated sugar and reserve.

Squeeze the juice into a small saucepan. Add the rest of the granulated sugar to the lemon juice in the saucepan and heat gently, stirring occasionally. When the sugar has dissolved, simmer gently for 3–4 minutes until syrupy.

With a cocktail stick or fine skewer prick the cake all over. Sprinkle the lemon zest and sugar over the top of the cake, drizzle over the syrup and leave to cool in the tin. Cut the cake into squares and serve.

Try this: FOR AN ALTERNATIVE: 252   FOR A COOKIE OR TRAYBAKE: 106

Carrot Cake

CUTS INTO 8 SLICES

200 g/7 oz plain flour
½ tsp ground cinnamon
½ tsp freshly grated nutmeg
1 tsp baking powder
1 tsp bicarbonate of soda
150 g/5 oz dark
   muscovado sugar

200 ml/7 fl oz vegetable oil
3 medium eggs
225 g/8 oz carrots, peeled
   and roughly grated
50 g/2 oz chopped walnuts

For the icing:
175 g/6 oz cream cheese
finely grated rind of
   1 orange
1 tbsp orange juice
1 tsp vanilla essence
125 g/4 oz icing sugar

Preheat the oven to 150°C/300°F/Gas Mark 2, 10 minutes before baking. Lightly oil and line the base of a deep 15 cm/6 inch square cake tin with greaseproof paper.

Sift the flour, spices, baking powder and bicarbonate of soda together into a large bowl. Stir in the dark muscovado sugar and mix together. Lightly whisk the oil and eggs together, then gradually stir into the flour and sugar mixture. Stir well.

Add the carrots and walnuts. Mix thoroughly, then pour into the prepared cake tin. Bake in the preheated oven for 1¼ hours, or until light and springy to the touch and a skewer inserted into the centre of the cake comes out clean.

Remove from the oven and allow to cool in the tin for 5 minutes before turning out on to a wire rack. Reserve until cold.

To make the icing, beat together the cream cheese, orange rind, orange juice and vanilla essence. Sift the icing sugar and stir into the cream cheese mixture.

When cold, discard the lining paper, spread the cream cheese icing over the top and serve cut into squares.

Try this: FOR AN ALTERNATIVE: 226 FOR A COOKIE OR TRAYBAKE: 50

Buttery Passion Fruit Madeira Cake

CUTS INTO 8-10 SLICES

210 g/7½ oz plain flour
1 tsp baking powder
175 g/6 oz unsalted
   butter, softened

250 g/9 oz caster sugar
grated zest of 1 orange
1 tsp vanilla essence
3 medium eggs, beaten

2 tbsp milk
6 ripe passion fruits
50 g/2 oz icing sugar
icing sugar, to dust

Preheat the oven to 180°C/350°F/Gas Mark 4, 10 minutes before baking. Lightly oil and line the base of a 23 x 12.5 cm/9 x 5 inch loaf tin with greaseproof paper. Sift the flour and baking powder into a bowl and reserve.

Beat the butter, sugar, orange zest and vanilla essence until light and fluffy, then gradually beat in the eggs, 1 tablespoon at a time, beating well after each addition. If the mixture appears to curdle or separate, beat in a little of the flour mixture.

Fold in the flour mixture with the milk until just blended. Do not over mix. Spoon lightly into the prepared tin and smooth the top evenly. Sprinkle lightly with an extra teaspoon of caster sugar.

Bake in the preheated oven for 55 minutes, or until well risen and golden brown. Remove from the oven and leave to cool for 15–20 minutes. Turn the cake out of the tin and discard the lining paper.

Cut the passion fruits in half and scoop out the pulp into a sieve set over a bowl. Press the juice through using a rubber spatula or wooden spoon. Stir in the icing sugar and stir to dissolve, adding a little extra sugar if necessary.

Using a skewer, pierce holes all over the cake. Slowly spoon the passion fruit glaze over the cake and allow to seep in. Gently invert the cake on to a wire rack, then turn it back the right way up. Dust with icing sugar and cool completely. Serve the Madeira cake cold.

Try this: FOR AN ALTERNATIVE: 208   FOR A COOKIE OR TRAYBAKE: 34

Whisked Sponge Cake

CUTS INTO 6 SLICES

125 g/4 oz plain flour, plus 1 tsp	3 medium eggs	50 g/2 oz fresh
175 g/6 oz caster sugar,	1 tsp vanilla essence	raspberries, crushed
plus 1 tsp	4 tbsp raspberry jam	icing sugar, to dust

Preheat the oven to 200°C/400°F/Gas Mark 6, 15 minutes before baking. Mix 1 teaspoon of the flour and 1 teaspoon of the sugar together. Lightly oil two 18 cm/7 inch sandwich tins and dust lightly with the sugar and flour.

Place the eggs in a large heatproof bowl. Add the sugar, then place over a saucepan of gently simmering water ensuring that the base of the bowl does not touch the hot water. Using an electric whisk beat the sugar and eggs until they become light and fluffy. The whisk should leave a trail in the mixture when it is lifted out.

Remove the bowl from the saucepan of water, add the vanilla essence and continue beating for 2–3 minutes. Sift the flour gently into the egg mixture and using a metal spoon or rubber spatula carefully fold in, taking care not to over mix and remove all the air that has been whisked in.

Divide the mixture between the two prepared cake tins. Tap lightly on the work surface to remove any air bubbles. Bake in the preheated oven for 20–25 minutes, or until golden. Test that the cake is ready by gently pressing the centre with a clean finger – it should spring back.

Leave to cool in the tins for 5 minutes, then turn out on to a wire rack. Blend the jam and the crushed raspberries together. When the cakes are cold spread over the jam mixture and sandwich together. Dust the top with icing sugar and serve.

Try this: FOR AN ALTERNATIVE: 198   FOR A COOKIE OR TRAYBAKE: 54

Victoria Sponge with Mango & Mascarpone

CUTS INTO 8 SLICES

175 g/6 oz caster sugar, plus
   extra for dusting
175 g/6 oz self-raising flour,
   plus extra for dusting

175 g/6 oz butter
   or margarine
3 large eggs
1 tsp vanilla essence

25 g/1 oz icing sugar
250 g/9 oz mascarpone
   cheese
1 large ripe mango, peeled

Preheat the oven to 190°C/375°F/Gas Mark 5, 10 minutes before baking. Lightly oil two 18 cm/7 inch sandwich tins and lightly dust with caster sugar and flour, tapping the tins to remove any excess.

In a large bowl cream the butter or margarine and sugar together with a wooden spoon until light and creamy. In another bowl mix the eggs and vanilla essence together. Sift the flour several times on to a plate. Beat a little egg into the butter and sugar, then a little flour and beat well.

Continue adding the flour and eggs alternately, beating between each addition, until the mixture is well mixed and smooth. Divide the mixture between the two prepared cake tins, level the surface, then using the back of a large spoon, make a slight dip in the centre of each cake.

Bake in the preheated oven for 25–30 minutes, until the centre of the cake springs back when gently pressed with a clean finger. Turn out on to a wire rack and leave the cakes until cold.

Beat the icing sugar and mascarpone cheese together, then chop the mango into small cubes. Use half the mascarpone and mango to sandwich the cakes together. Spread the rest of the mascarpone on top, decorate with the remaining mango and serve. Otherwise lightly cover and store in the refrigerator. Use within 3–4 days.

Try this: FOR AN ALTERNATIVE: 194 FOR A COOKIE OR TRAYBAKE: 104

Fresh Strawberry Sponge Cake

8-10 SERVINGS

175 g/6 oz unsalted
  butter, softened
175 g/6 oz caster sugar
1 tsp vanilla essence

3 large eggs, beaten
175 g/6 oz self-raising flour
150 ml/¼ pint double cream
2 tbsp icing sugar, sifted

225 g/8 oz fresh strawberries,
  hulled and chopped
few extra strawberries,
  to decorate

Preheat the oven to 190°C/375°F/Gas Mark 5, 10 minutes before baking. Lightly oil and line the bases of two 20.5 cm/8 inch round cake tins with greaseproof paper.

Using an electric whisk, beat the butter, sugar and vanilla essence until pale and fluffy. Gradually beat in the eggs a little at a time, beating well between each addition. Sift half the flour over the mixture and, using a metal spoon or rubber spatula, gently fold into the mixture. Sift over the remaining flour and fold in until just blended.

Divide the mixture between the tins, spreading evenly. Gently smooth the surfaces with the back of a spoon. Bake in the centre of the preheated oven for 20–25 minutes, or until well risen and golden.

Remove and leave to cool before turning out on to a wire rack. Whip the cream with 1 tablespoon of the icing sugar until it forms soft peaks. Fold in the chopped strawberries.

Spread one cake layer evenly with the mixture and top with the second cake layer, rounded side up. Thickly dust the cake with icing sugar and decorate with the reserved strawberries. Carefully slide on to a serving plate and serve.

Try this: FOR AN ALTERNATIVE: 232   FOR A COOKIE OR TRAYBAKE: 160

Swiss Roll

CUTS INTO 8 SLICES

75 g/3 oz self-raising flour
3 large eggs
1 tsp vanilla essence
90 g/3½ oz caster sugar

25 g/1 oz hazelnuts, toasted
and finely chopped
3 tbsp apricot conserve
300 ml/½ pint double cream,

lightly whipped
50 g/2 oz icing sugar
1–1½ tbsp lemon juice

Preheat the oven to 220°C/425°F/Gas Mark 7, 15 minutes before baking. Lightly oil and line the base of a 23 x 33 cm/9 x 13 inch Swiss roll tin with a single sheet of greaseproof or baking paper. Sift the flour several times, then reserve on top of the oven to warm a little.

Place a mixing bowl with the eggs, vanilla essence and sugar over a saucepan of hot water, ensuring that the base of the bowl is not touching the water. With the saucepan off the heat, whisk with an electric hand whisk until the egg mixture becomes pale and mousse-like and has increased in volume.

Remove the basin from the saucepan and continue to whisk for a further 2–3 minutes. Sift in the flour and very gently fold in using a metal spoon or rubber spatula, being careful not to knock out the air whisked in already. Pour into the prepared tin, tilting to ensure that the mixture is evenly distributed. Bake in the preheated oven for 10–12 minutes, or until well risen, golden brown and the top springs back when touched lightly with a clean finger.

Sprinkle the toasted, chopped hazelnuts over a large sheet of greaseproof paper. When the cake has cooked, turn out on to the hazelnut covered paper and trim the edges of the cake. Holding an edge of the paper with the short side of the cake nearest you, roll the cake up.

When fully cold, carefully unroll and spread with the jam and then the cream. Roll back up and serve. Otherwise, store in the refrigerator and eat within two days.

Try this: FOR AN ALTERNATIVE: 262   FOR A COOKIE OR TRAYBAKE: 122

Chestnut Cake

SERVES 8–10

175 g/6 oz butter, softened	175 g/6 oz plain flour	50 g/2 oz pine nuts, toasted
175 g/6 oz caster sugar	1 tsp baking powder	125 g/4 oz icing sugar
250 g can sweetened chestnut purée	pinch of ground cloves	5 tbsp lemons juice
3 medium eggs, lightly beaten	1 tsp fennel seeds, crushed	pared strips of lemon rind, to decorate
	75 g/3 oz raisins	

Preheat oven to 150°C/300°F/Gas Mark 2. Oil and line a 23 cm/9 inch springform tin. Beat together the butter and sugar until light and fluffy. Add the chestnut purée and beat. Gradually add the eggs, beating after each addition. Sift in the flour with the baking powder and cloves. Add the fennel seeds and beat. The mixture should drop easily from a wooden spoon when tapped against the side of the bowl. If not, add a little milk.

Beat in the raisins and pine nuts. Spoon the mixture into the prepared tin and smooth the top. Transfer to the centre of the oven and bake in the preheated oven for 55–60 minutes, or until a skewer inserted in the centre of the cake comes out clean. Remove from the oven and leave in the tin.

Meanwhile, mix together the icing sugar and lemon juice in a small saucepan until smooth. Heat gently until hot, but not boiling. Using a cocktail stick or skewer, poke holes into the cake all over. Pour the hot syrup evenly over the cake and leave to soak into the cake. Decorate with pared strips of lemon and serve.

Try this: FOR AN ALTERNATIVE: 238   FOR A COOKIE OR TRAYBAKE 70

Almond Cake

CUTS INTO 8 SLICES

225 g/8 oz butter or
   margarine
225 g/8 oz caster sugar
3 large eggs

1 tsp vanilla essence
1 tsp almond essence
125 g/4 oz self-raising flour
175 g/6 oz ground almonds

50 g/2 oz whole
   almonds, blanched
25 g/1 oz plain dark
   chocolate

Preheat the oven to 150°C/300°F/Gas Mark 2. Lightly oil and line the base of a 20.5 cm/ 8 inch deep round cake tin with greaseproof or baking paper.

Cream together the butter or margarine and sugar with a wooden spoon until light and fluffy. Beat the eggs and essences together. Gradually add to the sugar and butter mixture and mix well between each addition.

Sift the flour and mix with the ground almonds. Beat into the egg mixture until mixed well and smooth. Pour into the prepared cake tin. Roughly chop the whole almonds and scatter over the cake.

Bake in the preheated oven for 45 minutes, or until golden and risen and a skewer inserted into the centre of the cake comes out clean. Remove from the tin and leave to cool on a wire rack.

Melt the chocolate in a small bowl placed over a saucepan of gently simmering water, stirring until smooth and free of lumps. Drizzle the melted chocolate over the cooled cake and serve once the chocolate has set.

Try this: FOR AN ALTERNATIVE: 224   FOR A COOKIE OR TRAYBAKE: 72

Coffee & Pecan Cake

CUTS INTO 8 SLICES

175 g/6 oz self-raising flour
125 g/4 oz butter or margarine
175 g/6 oz golden caster sugar
1 tbsp instant coffee
    powder or granules
2 large eggs

50 g/2 oz pecans,
    roughly chopped

For the icing:
1 tsp instant coffee powder
    or granules

1 tsp cocoa powder
75 g/3 oz unsalted
    butter, softened
175 g/6 oz icing sugar, sifted
whole pecans, to decorate

Preheat the oven to 190°C/375°F/Gas Mark 5, 10 minutes before baking. Lightly oil and line the bases of two 18 cm/7 inch sandwich tins with greaseproof paper. Sift the flour and reserve.

Beat the butter or margarine and sugar together until light and creamy. Dissolve the coffee in 2 tablespoons of hot water and allow to cool. Lightly mix the eggs with the coffee liquid. Gradually beat into the creamed butter and sugar, adding a little of the sifted flour with each addition.

Fold in the pecans, then divide the mixture between the prepared tins and bake in the preheated oven for 20–25 minutes, or until well risen and firm to the touch. Leave to cool in the tins for 5 minutes before turning out and cooling on a wire rack.

To make the icing, blend together the coffee and cocoa powder with enough boiling water to make a stiff paste. Beat into the butter and icing sugar.

Sandwich the two cakes together using half of the icing. Spread the remaining icing over the top of the cake and decorate with the whole pecans to serve. Store in an airtight tin.

Try this: FOR AN ALTERNATIVE: 264   FOR A COOKIE OR TRAYBAKE: 66

Honey Cake

CUTS INTO 8-10 SLICES

50 g/2 oz butter
25 g/1 oz caster sugar
125 g/4 oz clear honey
175 g/6 oz plain flour

½ tsp bicarbonate of soda
½ tsp mixed spice
1 medium egg
2 tbsp milk

25 g/1 oz flaked almonds
1 tbsp clear honey,
  to drizzle

Preheat the oven to 180°C/350°F/Gas Mark 4, 10 minutes before baking. Lightly oil and line the base of an 18 cm/7 inch deep round cake tin with lightly oiled greaseproof or baking paper.

In a saucepan gently heat the butter, sugar and honey until the butter has just melted.

Sift the flour, bicarbonate of soda and mixed spice together into a bowl.

Beat the egg and the milk until mixed thoroughly.

Make a well in the centre of the sifted flour and pour in the melted butter and honey. Using a wooden spoon, beat well, gradually drawing in the flour from the sides of the bowl. When all the flour has been beaten in, add the egg mixture and mix thoroughly. Pour into the prepared tin and sprinkle with the flaked almonds.

Bake in the preheated oven for 30–35 minutes, or until well risen and golden brown and a skewer inserted into the centre of the cake comes out clean.

Remove from the oven, cool for a few minutes in the tin before turning out, and leave to cool on a wire rack. Drizzle with the remaining tablespoon of honey and serve.

Try this: FOR AN ALTERNATIVE: 180 FOR A COOKIE OR TRAYBAKE: 80

Gingerbread

CUTS INTO 8 SLICES

175 g/6 oz butter or margarine
225 g/8 oz black treacle
50 g/2 oz dark
   muscovado sugar

350 g/12 oz plain flour
2 tsp ground ginger
150 ml/¼ pint milk, warmed
2 medium eggs

1 tsp bicarbonate of soda
1 piece of stem ginger
  in syrup
1 tbsp stem ginger syrup

Preheat the oven to 150°C/300°C/Gas Mark 2, 10 minutes before baking. Lightly oil and line the base of a deep 20.5 cm/8 inch round cake tin with greaseproof paper.

In a saucepan gently heat the butter or margarine, black treacle and sugar, stirring occasionally until the butter melts. Leave to cool slightly.

Sift the flour and ground ginger into a large bowl. Make a well in the centre, then pour in the treacle mixture. Reserve 1 tablespoon of the milk, then pour the rest into the treacle mixture. Stir together lightly until mixed. Beat the eggs together, then stir into the mixture.

Dissolve the bicarbonate of soda in the remaining 1 tablespoon of warmed milk and add to the mixture. Beat the mixture until well mixed and free of lumps.

Pour into the prepared tin and bake in the preheated oven for 1 hour, or until well risen and a skewer inserted into the centre comes out clean.

Cool in the tin, then remove. Slice the stem ginger into thin slivers and sprinkle over the cake. Drizzle with the syrup and serve.

Try this: FOR AN ALTERNATIVE: 156 FOR A COOKIE OR TRAYBAKE: 62

Chocolate & Coconut Cake

CUTS INTO 8 SLICES

125 g/4 oz plain dark
  chocolate, roughly
  chopped
175 g/6 oz butter or
  margarine
175 g/6 oz caster sugar
3 medium eggs, beaten

15 g/6 oz self-raising flour
1 tbsp cocoa powder
50 g/2 oz desiccated coconut

For the icing:
125 g/4 oz butter
  or margarine

2 tbsp creamed coconut
225 g/8 oz icing sugar
25 g/1 oz desiccated
  coconut, lightly toasted

Preheat the oven to 180°C/350°F/Gas Mark 4, 10 minutes before baking. Melt the chocolate in a small bowl placed over a saucepan of gently simmering water, ensuring that the base of the bowl does not touch the water. When the chocolate has melted, stir until smooth and allow to cool.

Lightly oil and line the bases of two 18 cm/7 inch sandwich tins with greaseproof paper. In a large bowl, beat the butter or margarine and sugar together with a wooden spoon until light and creamy. Beat in the eggs a little at a time, then stir in the melted chocolate.

Sift the flour and cocoa powder together and gently fold into the chocolate mixture with a metal spoon or rubber spatula. Add the desiccated coconut and mix lightly. Divide between the two prepared tins and smooth the tops. Bake in the preheated oven for 25–30 minutes, or until a skewer comes out clean when inserted into the centre of the cake. Allow to cool in the tin for 5 minutes, then turn out, discard the lining paper and leave on a wire rack until cold.

Beat together the butter or margarine and creamed coconut until light. Add the icing sugar and mix well. Spread half of the icing on one cake and press the cakes together. Spread the remaining icing over the top, sprinkle with the coconut and serve.

 Try this: FOR AN ALTERNATIVE: 252 FOR A COOKIE OR TRAYBAKE: 78

Double Chocolate Cake with Cinnamon

CUTS INTO 10 SLICES

50 g/2 oz cocoa powder
1 tsp ground cinnamon
225 g/8 oz self-raising flour
225 g/8 oz unsalted butter
or margarine
225 g/8 oz caster sugar
4 large eggs

For the filling:
125 g/4 oz white chocolate
50 ml/2 fl oz double cream
25 g/1 oz plain dark chocolate

Preheat the oven to 190°C/375°F/Gas Mark 5, 10 minutes before baking. Lightly oil and line the base of two 20.5 cm/8 inch sandwich tins with greaseproof or baking paper. Sift the cocoa powder, cinnamon and flour together and reserve.

In a large bowl, cream the butter or margarine and sugar until light and fluffy. Beat in the eggs a little at a time until they are all incorporated and the mixture is smooth. If it looks curdled at any point beat in 1 tablespoon of the sifted flour. Using a rubber spatula or metal spoon, fold the sifted flour and cocoa powder into the egg mixture until mixed well.

Divide between the two prepared cake tins, and level the surface. Bake in the preheated oven for 25–30 minutes, until springy to the touch and a skewer inserted into the centre of the cake comes out clean. Turn out on to a wire rack to cool.

To make the filling, coarsely break the white chocolate and heat the cream very gently in a small saucepan. Add the broken chocolate, stirring until melted. Leave to cool, then using half of the cooled white chocolate sandwich the cakes together.

Top the cake with the remaining cooled white chocolate. Coarsely grate the dark chocolate over the top and serve.

Try this: FOR AN ALTERNATIVE: 178 FOR A COOKIE OR TRAYBAKE: 52

Chocolate Orange Fudge Cake

CUTS INTO 8-10 SLICES

60 g/2½ oz cocoa powder
grated zest of 1 orange
350 g/12 oz self-raising flour
2 tsp baking powder
1 tsp bicarbonate of soda
½ tsp salt

225 g/8 oz light soft
   brown sugar
175 g/6 oz butter, softened
3 medium eggs
1 tsp vanilla essence
250 ml/9 fl oz soured cream

6 tbsp butter
6 tbsp milk
thinly pared rind of 1 orange
6 tbsp cocoa powder
250 g/9 oz icing
   sugar, sifted

Preheat the oven to 180°C/350°F/Gas Mark 4, 10 minutes before baking. Lightly oil and line two 23 cm/9 inch round cake tins with non-stick baking parchment.

Blend the cocoa powder and 50 ml/2 fl oz of boiling water until smooth. Stir in the orange zest and reserve. Sift together the flour, baking powder, bicarbonate of soda and salt, then reserve. Cream together the sugar and softened butter and beat in the eggs, one at a time, then the cocoa mixture and vanilla essence. Finally, stir in the flour mixture and the soured cream in alternate spoonfuls.

Divide the mixture between the prepared tins and bake in the preheated oven for 35 minutes, or until the edges of the cake pull away from the tin and the tops spring back when lightly pressed. Cool in the tins for 10 minutes, then turn out onto wire racks until cold.

Gently heat together the butter and milk with the pared orange rind. Simmer for 10 minutes, stirring occasionally. Remove from the heat and discard the orange rind.

Pour the warm orange and milk mixture into a large bowl and stir in the cocoa powder. Gradually beat in the sifted icing sugar and beat until the icing is smooth and spreadable. Place one cake onto a large serving plate. Top with about one quarter of the icing, place the second cake on top, then cover the cake completely with the remaining icing. Serve.

Try this: FOR AN ALTERNATIVE: 172 FOR A COOKIE OR TRAYBAKE: 82

Cream Cakes & Special Occasions

Marzipan Cake

SERVES 12-14

450 g/1 lb blanched almonds
300 g/11 oz icing sugar
  (includes sugar for
  dusting and rolling)
4 medium egg whites
125 g/4 oz Madeira cake

2 tbsp Marsala wine
225 g/8 oz ricotta cheese
50 g/2 oz caster sugar
grated zest of 1 lemon
50 g/2 oz candied peel,
  finely chopped

25 g/1 oz glacé cherries,
  finely chopped
425 g can peach halves,
  drained
200 ml/⅓ pint double cream

Grind the blanched almonds in a food processor until fairly fine. Mix with 200 g/7 oz of the icing sugar. Beat the egg whites until stiff then fold into the almond mixture using a metal spoon or rubber spatula to form a stiffish dough. It will still be quite sticky but will firm up as it rests. Leave for 30 minutes.

Dust a work surface very generously with some of the remaining icing sugar so that the marzipan does not stick. Roll out two-thirds of the marzipan into a large sheet to a thickness of about 5 mm/1/4 inch. Use to line a sloping-sided baking dish with a base measuring 25.5 cm x 20.5 cm/10 x 8 inches. Trim the edges and put any trimmings with the remainder of the marzipan.

Cut the Madeira cake into thin slices and make a layer of sponge to cover the bottom of the marzipan. Sprinkle with the Marsala wine. Beat the ricotta with the sugar and add the lemon zest, candied peel and cherries. Spread this over the sponge. Slice the peaches and put them on top of the ricotta. Whip the cream and spread it over the peaches. Roll out the remaining marzipan and lay it over the cream to seal the whole cake, pressing down gently to remove any air. Press the edges of the marzipan together. Chill in the refrigerator for 2 hours.

Turn the cake out on to a serving plate and dust generously with icing sugar. Slice thickly and serve immediately.

Try this: FOR AN ALTERNATIVE: 220 FOR A COOKIE OR TRAYBAKE: 60

Sauternes &
Olive Oil Cake

SERVES 8–10

125 g/4 oz plain flour, plus
    extra for dusting
4 medium eggs
125 g/4 oz caster sugar
grated zest of ½ lemon

grated zest of ½ orange
2 tbsp Sauternes or other
    sweet dessert wine
3 tbsp very best quality
    extra-virgin olive oil

4 ripe peaches
1–2 tsp soft brown sugar, or
    to taste
1 tbsp lemon juice
icing sugar, to dust

Preheat the oven to 140°C/275°F/Gas Mark 1. Oil and line a 25.5 cm/10 inch springform tin. Sift the flour on to a large sheet of greaseproof paper and reserve. Using a freestanding electric mixer, if possible, whisk the eggs and sugar together, until pale and stiff. Add the lemon and orange zest.

Turn the speed to low and pour the flour from the paper in a slow, steady stream on to the eggs and sugar mixture. Immediately add the wine and olive oil and switch the machine off as the olive oil should not be incorporated completely.

Using a rubber spatula, fold the mixture very gently 3 or 4 times so that the ingredients are just incorporated. Pour the mixture immediately into the prepared tin and bake in the preheated oven for 20–25 minutes, without opening the door for at least 15 minutes. Test if cooked by pressing the top lightly with a clean finger – if it springs back, remove from the oven, if not, bake for a little longer.

Leave the cake to cool in the tin on a wire rack. Remove the cake from the tin when cool enough to handle.

Meanwhile, skin the peaches and cut into segments. Toss with the brown sugar and lemon juice and reserve. When the cake is cold, dust generously with icing sugar, cut into wedges and serve with the peaches.

Apricot & Almond Layer Cake

CUTS INTO 8–10 SLICES

150 g/5 oz unsalted
butter, softened
125 g/4 oz caster sugar
5 medium eggs, separated
150 g/5 oz plain dark
chocolate, melted

and cooled
150 g/5 oz self-raising
flour, sifted
50 g/2 oz ground almonds
75 g/3 oz icing sugar, sifted
300 g/11 oz apricot jam

1 tbsp amaretto liqueur
125 g/4 oz unsalted butter,
melted
125 g/4 oz plain dark
chocolate, melted

Preheat the oven to 180°C/350°F/Gas Mark 4, 10 minutes before baking. Lightly oil and line 2 x 23 cm/9 inch round cake tins. Cream the butter and sugar together until light and fluffy, then beat in the egg yolks, one at a time, beating well after each addition. Stir in the cooled chocolate with 1 tablespoon of cooled boiled water, then fold in the flour and ground almonds.

Whisk the egg whites until stiff, then gradually whisk in the icing sugar beating well after each addition. Whisk until the egg whites are stiff and glossy, then fold the egg whites into the chocolate mixture in 2 batches. Divide the mixture evenly between the prepared tins and bake in the preheated oven for 30–40 minutes or until firm. Leave for 5 minutes before turning out onto wire racks. Leave to cool completely.

Split the cakes in half. Gently heat the jam, pass through a sieve and stir in the amaretto liqueur. Place 1 cake layer onto a serving plate. Spread with a little of the jam, then sandwich with the next layer. Repeat with all the layers and use any remaining jam to brush over the entire cake. Leave until the jam sets.

Meanwhile, beat the butter and chocolate together until smooth, then cool at room temperature until thick enough to spread. Cover the top and sides of the cake with the chocolate icing and leave to set before slicing and serving.

Try this: FOR AN ALTERNATIVE: 204   FOR A COOKIE OR TRAYBAKE: 104

Luxury Carrot Cake

CUTS INTO 12 SLICES

275 g/10 oz plain flour
2 tsp baking powder
1 tsp bicarbonate of soda
1 tsp salt
2 tsp ground cinnamon
1 tsp ground ginger
200 g/7 oz dark soft
    brown sugar
100 g/3½ oz caster sugar

4 large eggs, beaten
250 ml/9 fl oz sunflower oil
1 tbsp vanilla essence
4 carrots, peeled and
    shredded (about 450 g/1 lb)
380 g/14 oz can crushed
    pineapple, well drained
125 g/4 oz pecans or walnuts,
    toasted and chopped

For the frosting:
175 g/6 oz cream cheese,
    softened
50 g/2 oz butter, softened
1 tsp vanilla essence
225 g/8 oz icing sugar, sifted
1–2 tbsp milk

Preheat the oven to 180°C/350°F/Gas Mark 4, 10 minutes before baking. Lightly oil a 33 x 23 cm /13 x 9 inch baking tin. Line the base with non-stick baking paper, oil and dust with flour.

Sift the first 6 ingredients into a large bowl and stir in the sugars to blend. Make a well in the centre. Beat the eggs, oil and vanilla essence together and pour into the well. Using an electric whisk, gradually beat drawing in the flour mixture from the side until a smooth batter forms.

Stir in the carrots, crushed pineapple and chopped nuts until blended. Pour into the prepared tin and smooth the surface evenly. Bake in the preheated oven for 50 minutes, or until firm and a skewer inserted into the centre comes out clean. Remove from the oven and leave to cool before removing from the tin and discarding the lining paper.

For the frosting, beat the cream cheese, butter and vanilla essence together until smooth, then gradually beat in the icing sugar until the frosting is smooth. Add a little milk, if necessary. Spread the frosting over the top. Refrigerate for about 1 hour to set the frosting, then cut into squares and serve.

Try this: FOR AN ALTERNATIVE: 190   FOR A COOKIE OR TRAYBAKE: 50

Autumn Bramley Apple Cake

CUTS INTO 8-10 SLICES

225 g/8 oz self-raising flour
1½ tsp baking powder
150 g/5 oz margarine, softened
150 g/5 oz caster sugar, plus

extra for sprinkling
1 tsp vanilla essence
2 large eggs, beaten
1.1 kg/2½ lbs Bramley cooking apples, peeled,

cored and sliced
1 tbsp lemon juice
½ tsp ground cinnamon
fresh custard or cream, to serve

Preheat the oven to 170°C/325°F/Gas Mark 3, 10 minutes before baking. Lightly oil and line the base of a deep 20.5 cm/8 inch cake tin with non-stick baking paper.

Sift the flour and baking powder into a small bowl. Beat the margarine, sugar and vanilla essence until light and fluffy. Gradually beat in the eggs a little at a time, beating well after each addition. Stir in the flour mixture.

Spoon about one-third of the mixture into the tin, smoothing the surface. Toss the apple slices in the lemon juice and cinnamon and spoon over the cake mixture, making a thick, even layer. Spread the remaining mixture over the apple layer to the edge of the tin, making sure the apples are covered. Smooth the top with the back of a wet spoon and sprinkle generously with sugar.

Bake in the preheated oven for 1½ hours, or until well risen and golden, the apples are tender and the centre of the cake springs back when pressed lightly. Reduce the oven temperature slightly and cover the cake loosely with tinfoil if the top browns too quickly.

Transfer to a wire rack and cool for about 20 minutes in the tin. Run a thin knife blade between the cake and the the tin to loosen the cake, and invert on to a paper-lined rack. Turn the cake the right way up and cool. Serve with the custard or cream.

Try this: FOR AN ALTERNATIVE: 178   FOR A COOKIE OR TRAYBAKE: 52

Celebration Fruit Cake

CUTS INTO 16 SLICES

125 g/4 oz butter or margarine
125 g/4 oz soft dark brown sugar
380 g can crushed pineapple
150 g/5 oz raisins
150 g/5 oz sultanas
125 g/4 oz crystallised
  ginger, finely chopped
125 g/4 oz glacé cherries,
  coarsely chopped
125 g/4 oz mixed cut peel
225 g/8 oz self-raising flour
1 tsp bicarbonate of soda
2 tsp mixed spice
1 tsp ground cinnamon
½ tsp salt
2 large eggs, beaten

For the topping:
100 g/3½ oz pecan or walnut
  halves, lightly toasted
125 g/4 oz red, green and
  yellow glacé cherries
100 g/3½ oz small pitted
  prunes or dates
2 tbsp clear honey

Preheat the oven to 170°C/325°F/Gas Mark 3, 10 minutes before baking. Heat the butter and sugar in a saucepan until the sugar has dissolved, stirring frequently. Add the pineapple and juice, dried fruits and peel. Bring to the boil and simmer for 3 minutes, stirring occasionally. Remove from the heat to cool completely.

Lightly oil and line the base of a 20.5 x 7.5 cm/8 x 3 inch loose-bottomed cake tin with non-stick baking paper. Sift the flour, bicarbonate of soda, spices and salt into a bowl. Add the boiled fruit mixture to the flour with the eggs and mix. Spoon into the tin and smooth the top.

Bake in the preheated oven for 1¼ hours, or until a skewer inserted into the centre comes out clean. If the cake is browning too quickly, cover loosely with tinfoil and reduce the oven temperature. Remove and cool completely before removing from the tin and discarding the lining paper.

Arrange the nuts, cherries and prunes or dates in an attractive pattern on top of the cake. Heat the honey and brush over the topping to glaze. Alternatively, toss the nuts and fruits in the warm honey and spread evenly over the top of the cake. Cool completely and store in a cake tin for a day or two before serving to allow the flavours to develop.

Try this: FOR AN ALTERNATIVE: 182   FOR A COOKIE OR TRAYBAKE: 116

Wild Strawberry & Rose Petal Jam Cake

CUTS INTO 8 SERVINGS

275 g/10 oz plain flour
1 tsp baking powder
¼ tsp salt
150 g/5 oz unsalted
    butter, softened
200 g/7 oz caster sugar
2 large eggs, beaten
2 tbsp rosewater

125 ml/4 fl oz milk
125 g/4 oz rose petal or
    strawberry jam,
    slightly warmed
125 g/4 oz wild strawberries,
    hulled, or baby
    strawberries, chopped
frosted rose petals, to decorate

For the rose cream filling:
200 ml/7 fl oz double cream
25 ml/1 fl oz natural
    Greek yogurt
2 tbsp rosewater
1–2 tbsp icing sugar

Preheat the oven to 180°C/350°F/Gas Mark 4, 10 minutes before baking. Lightly oil and flour a 20.5 cm/8 inch non-stick cake tin.

Sift the flour, baking powder and salt into a bowl and reserve. In another bowl, beat the butter and sugar until light and fluffy. Beat in the eggs, a little at a time, then stir in the rosewater. Gently fold in the flour mixture and milk with a metal spoon or rubber spatula and mix lightly together. Spoon the cake mixture into the tin, spreading evenly and smoothing the top.

Bake in the preheated oven for 25–30 minutes, or until well risen and golden and the centre springs back when pressed with a clean finger. Remove and cool, then remove from the tin.

For the filling, whisk the cream, yogurt, 1 tablespoon of rosewater and 1 tablespoon of icing sugar until soft peaks form. Split the cake horizontally in half and sprinkle with the remaining rosewater. Spread the warmed jam on the base of the cake. Top with half the whipped cream mixture, then sprinkle with half the strawberries. Place the remaining cake half on top. Spread with the remaining cream and swirl, if desired. Decorate with the rose petals. Dust the cake lightly with a little icing sugar and serve.

Try this: FOR AN ALTERNATIVE: 198   FOR A COOKIE OR TRAYBAKE: 104

Fruity Roulade

SERVES 4

For the sponge:
3 medium eggs
75 g/3 oz caster sugar
75 g/3 oz plain flour, sieved
1–2 tbsp caster sugar
   for sprinkling

For the filling:
125 g/4 oz Quark
125 g/4 oz half-fat
   Greek yogurt
25 g/1 oz caster sugar
1 tbsp orange

liqueur (optional)
grated rind of 1 orange
125 g/4 oz strawberries,
   hulled and cut
   into quarters, plus extra
   to decorate

Preheat the oven to 220°C/425°F/Gas Mark 7. Lightly oil and line a 33 x 23 cm/13 x 9 inch Swiss roll tin with greaseproof paper.

Using an electric whisk, whisk the eggs and sugar until the mixture is doubled in volume and leaves a trail across the top. Fold in the flour with a metal spoon or rubber spatula. Pour into the prepared tin and bake in the preheated oven for 10–12 minutes, until well risen and golden.

Place a whole sheet of greaseproof paper on a flat work surface and sprinkle evenly with caster sugar.

Turn the cooked sponge out on to the paper, discard the paper, trim the sponge and roll up encasing the paper inside. Reserve until cool.

To make the filling, mix together the Quark, yogurt, caster sugar, liqueur (if using) and orange rind. Unroll the roulade and spread over the mixture. Scatter over the strawberries and roll up. Decorate the roulade with the strawberries. Dust with the icing sugar and serve.

Try this: FOR AN ALTERNATIVE: 200 FOR A COOKIE OR TRAYBAKE: 100

Raspberry & Hazelnut Meringue Cake

CUTS INTO 8 SERVINGS

For the meringue:
4 large egg whites
¼ tsp cream of tartar
225 g/8 oz caster sugar
75 g/3 oz hazelnuts, skinned,
  toasted and finely ground

For the filling:
300 ml/½ pint double cream
1 tbsp icing sugar
1–2 tbsp raspberry-flavoured
  liqueur (optional)
350 g/12 oz fresh raspberries

Preheat the oven to 140°C/275°F/Gas Mark 1. Line two baking sheets with non-stick baking paper and draw a 20.5 cm/8 inch circle on each.

Whisk the egg whites and cream of tartar until soft peaks form then gradually beat in the sugar, 2 tablespoons at a time. Beat well after each addition until the whites are stiff and glossy. Using a metal spoon or rubber spatula, gently fold in the ground hazelnuts.

Divide the mixture evenly between the two circles and spread neatly. Swirl one of the circles to make a decorative top layer. Bake in the preheated oven for about 1½ hours, until crisp and dry. Turn off the oven and allow the meringues to cool for 1 hour. Transfer to a wire rack to cool completely. Carefully peel off the papers.

For the filling, whip the cream, icing sugar and liqueur, if using, together until soft peaks form. Place the flat round on a serving plate. Spread over most of the cream, reserving some for decorating, and arrange the raspberries in concentric circles over the cream.

Place the swirly meringue on top of the cream and raspberries, pressing down gently. Pipe the remaining cream on to the meringue, decorate with a few raspberries and serve.

Try this: FOR AN ALTERNATIVE: 238   FOR A COOKIE OR TRAYBAKE: 40

Hazelnut, Chocolate & Chestnut Meringue Torte

SERVES 8–10

For the chocolate meringue:
1 medium egg white
50 g/2 oz caster sugar
2 tbsp cocoa powder

For the hazelnut meringue:
75 g/3 oz hazelnuts, toasted

2 medium egg whites
125 g/4 oz caster sugar

For the filling:
300 ml/½ pint double cream
250 g can sweetened
    chestnut purée

50 g/2 oz plain dark
    chocolate, melted
25 g/1 oz plain dark
    chocolate, grated

Preheat oven to 130°C/250°F/Gas Mark 1⁄2. Line 3 baking sheets with non-stick baking parchment and draw a 20.5 cm/8 inch circle on each. Beat 1 egg white until stiff peaks form. Add 25 g/1 oz of the sugar and beat until shiny. Mix the cocoa with the remaining 25 g/1 oz of sugar and add 1 tablespoon at a time, beating well after each addition, until all the sugar is added and the mixture is stiff and glossy. Spread on to 1 of the baking sheets within the circle drawn on the underside.

Put the hazelnuts in a food processor and blend until chopped. In a clean bowl, beat the 2 egg whites until stiff. Add 50 g/2 oz of the sugar and beat. Add the remaining sugar about 1 tablespoon at a time, beating after each addition until all the sugar is added and the mixture is stiff and glossy. Reserve 2 tablespoons of the nuts, then fold in the remainder and divide between the 2 remaining baking sheets. Sprinkle one of the hazelnut meringues with the reserved hazelnuts and transfer all the baking sheets to the oven. Bake in the preheated oven for 1½ hours. Turn the oven off and leave in the oven until cold.

Whip the cream until thick. Beat the chestnut purée in another bowl until soft. Add a spoonful of the cream and fold together before adding the remaining cream and melted chocolate and fold together. Place the plain hazelnut meringue on a serving plate. Top with half the cream and chestnut mixture. Add the chocolate meringue and top with the remaining cream. Add the final meringue. Sprinkle over the grated chocolate and serve.

Try this: FOR AN ALTERNATIVE: 236   FOR A COOKIE OR TRAYBAKE: 70

Chocolate Hazelnut Meringue Gateau

CUTS INTO 8–10 SLICES

5 medium egg whites
275 g/10 oz caster sugar
125 g/4 oz hazelnuts, toasted
    and finely chopped
175 g/6 oz plain

dark chocolate
100 g/3½ oz butter
3 medium eggs, separated
    plus 1 medium egg white
25 g/1 oz icing sugar

125 ml/4 fl oz double cream
hazelnuts, toasted and
    chopped, to decorate

Preheat the oven to 150°C/300°F/Gas Mark 2, 5 minutes before baking. Cut three pieces of non-stick baking parchment into 30.5 x 12.5 cm/12 x 5 inch rectangles and then place onto two or three baking sheets.

Whisk the egg whites until stiff, add half the sugar and whisk until the mixture is stiff, smooth and glossy. Whisk in the remaining sugar, 1 tablespoon at a time, beating well between each addition. When all the sugar has been added whisk for 1 minute. Stir in the hazelnuts. Spoon the meringue inside the marked rectangles spreading in a continuous backwards and forwards movement. Bake in the preheated oven for 1¼ hours, remove and leave until cold. Trim the meringues until they measure 25.5 x 10 cm/10 x 4 inches. Reserve all the trimmings.

Melt the chocolate and the butter in a heatproof bowl set over a saucepan of gently simmering water and stir until smooth. Remove from the heat and beat in the egg yolks. Whisk the egg whites until stiff, then whisk in the icing sugar a little at a time. Fold the egg whites into the chocolate mixture and chill in the refrigerator for 20–30 minutes, until thick enough to spread. Whip the double cream until soft peaks form. Reserve.

Place one of the meringue layers onto a serving plate. Spread with about half of the mousse mixture, then top with a second meringue layer. Spread the remaining mouse mixture over the top with the third meringue. Spread the cream over the top and sprinkle with the chopped hazelnuts. Chill in the refrigerator for at least 4 hours. Serve cut into slices.

Try this: FOR AN ALTERNATIVE: 238   FOR A COOKIE OR TRAYBAKE: 66

Chocolate & Almond Daquoise with Summer Berries

CUTS INTO 8 SLICES

For the almond meringues:
6 large egg whites
¼ tsp cream of tartar
275 g/10 oz caster sugar
1/2 tsp almond essence
50 g/2 oz blanched or flaked
   almonds, lightly toasted
   and finely ground

**For the chocolate
   buttercream:**
75 g/3 oz butter, softened
450 g/1 lb icing sugar, sifted
50 g/2 oz cocoa powder,
   sifted
3–4 tbsp milk or single
   cream

550 g/1¼ lb mixed summer
   berries such as
   raspberries, strawberries
   and blackberries

To decorate:
toasted flaked almonds
icing sugar

Preheat the oven to 140°C/ 275°F/Gas Mark 1 10 minutes before baking. Line 3 baking sheets with non-stick baking paper and draw a 20.5 cm/8 inch round on each one.

Whisk the egg whites and cream of tartar until soft peaks form. Gradually beat in the sugar, 2 tablespoons at a time, beating well after each addition, until the whites are stiff and glossy.

Beat in the almond essence, then using a metal spoon or rubber spatula gently fold in the ground almonds. Divide the mixture evenly between the 3 circles of baking paper, spreading neatly into the rounds and smoothing the tops evenly. Bake in the preheated oven for about 1¼ hours or until crisp, rotating the baking sheets halfway through cooking. Turn off the oven, allow to cool for about 1 hour, then remove and cool completely before discarding the lining paper.

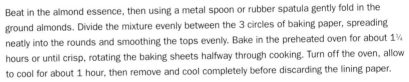

Beat the butter, icing sugar and cocoa powder until smooth and creamy, adding the milk or cream to form a soft consistency. Reserve about a quarter of the berries to decorate. Spread 1 meringue with a third of the buttercream and top with a third of the remaining berries. Repeat with the other meringue rounds, buttercream and berries. Scatter with the toasted flaked almonds, the reserved berries and sprinkle with icing sugar and serve.

Try this: FOR AN ALTERNATIVE: 224   FOR A COOKIE OR TRAYBAKE: 58

Peach & White Chocolate Gateau

CUTS INTO 8-10 SLICES

175 g/6 oz unsalted
  butter, softened
2 tsp grated orange rind
175 g/6 oz caster sugar
3 medium eggs
100 g/3½ oz white chocolate,
  melted and cooled

225 g/8 oz self-raising
  flour, sifted
300 ml/½ pint double cream
40 g/1½ oz icing sugar
125 g/4 oz hazelnuts, toasted
  and chopped

For the peach filling:
2 ripe peaches, peeled and
  chopped
2 tbsp peach or orange
  liqueur
300 ml/½ pint double cream
40 g/1½ oz icing sugar

Preheat the oven to 170°C/325°F/Gas Mark 3, 10 minutes before baking. Lightly oil and line a deep 23 cm/9 inch round cake tin. Cream the butter, orange rind and sugar together until light and fluffy. Add the eggs, one at a time, beating well after each addition, then beat in the cooled white chocolate. Add the flour and 175 ml/6 fl oz of water in two batches. Spoon into the prepared tin and bake in the preheated oven for 1½ hours or until firm. Leave to stand for at least 5 minutes before turning out onto a wire rack to cool completely.

To make the filling, place the peaches in a bowl and pour over the liqueur. Leave to stand for 30 minutes. Whip the cream with the icing sugar until soft peaks form, then fold in the peach mixture. Split the cold cake in to three layers, place one layer on a serving plate and spread with half the peach filling. Top with a second sponge layer and spread with the remaining peach filling. Top with the remaining cake.

Whip the cream and icing sugar together until soft peaks form. Spread over the top and sides of the cake, piping some onto the top if liked. Press the hazelnuts into the side of cake and if liked sprinkle a few on top. Chill in the refrigerator until required. Serve cut into slices. Store the cake in the refrigerator.

Try this: FOR AN ALTERNATIVE: 256 FOR A COOKIE OR TRAYBAKE: 140

White Chocolate & Raspberry Mousse Gateau

CUTS 8 SLICES

4 medium eggs
125 g/4 oz caster sugar
75 g/3 oz plain flour, sifted
25 g/1 oz cornflour, sifted
3 gelatine leaves
450 g/1 lb raspberries,

thawed if frozen
400 g/14 oz white chocolate
200 g/7 oz plain
fromage frais
2 medium egg whites
25 g/1 oz caster sugar

4 tbsp raspberry or
orange liqueur
200 ml/7 fl oz double cream
fresh raspberries, halved,
to decorate

Preheat the oven to 190°C/375°F/Gas Mark 5, 10 minutes before baking. Oil and line two 23 cm/9 inch cake tins. Whisk the eggs and sugar until thick and creamy and the whisk leaves a trail in the mixture. Fold in the flour and cornflour, then divide between the tins. Bake in the preheated oven for 12–15 minutes or until risen and firm. Cool in the tins, then turn out onto wire racks. Place the gelatine with 4 tablespoons of cold water in a dish and leave to soften for 5 minutes. Purée half the raspberries, press through a sieve, then heat until nearly boiling. Squeeze out excess water from the gelatine, add to the purée and stir until dissolved.

Melt 175 g/6 oz of the chocolate in a bowl set over a saucepan of simmering water. Leave to cool, then stir in the fromage frais and purée. Whisk the egg whites until stiff and whisk in the sugar. Fold into the raspberry mixture with the rest of the raspberries. Line the sides of a 23 cm/9 inch springform tin with non-stick baking parchment. Place one layer of sponge in the base and sprinkle with half the liqueur. Pour in the raspberry mixture and top with the second sponge. Brush with the remaining liqueur. Press down and chill in the refrigerator for 4 hours. Unmould onto a plate.

Cut a strip of double thickness non-stick baking paper to fit around the cake and stand 1 cm/½ inch higher. Melt the remaining white chocolate and spread thickly onto the paper. Leave until just setting. Wrap around the cake and freeze for 15 minutes. Peel away the paper. Whip the cream until thick and spread over the top. Decorate with raspberries and serve.

Try this: FOR AN ALTERNATIVE: 254   FOR A COOKIE OR TRAYBAKE: 54

Orange Fruit Cake

CUTS INTO 10-12 SLICES

For the cake:
225 g/8 oz self-raising flour
2 tsp baking powder
225 g/8 oz caster sugar
225 g/8 oz butter, softened
4 large eggs
grated zest of 1 orange
2 tbsp orange juice
2–3 tbsp Cointreau

125 g/4 oz chopped nuts
Cape gooseberries,
 blueberries, raspberries
 and mint sprigs to
 decorate
icing sugar, to dust (optional)

For the filling:
450 ml/¾ pint double cream

50 ml/2 fl oz Greek yogurt
½ tsp vanilla essence
2–3 tbsp Cointreau
1 tbsp icing sugar
450 g/1 lb orange fruits, such
 as mango, peach,
 nectarine, papaya and
 yellow plums

Preheat the oven to 180°C/350°F/Gas Mark 4, 10 minutes before baking. Line the base of a 25.5 cm/10 inch ring mould tin or deep springform tin with non-stick baking paper. Sift the flour and baking powder into a large bowl and stir in the sugar. Make a well in the centre and add the butter, eggs, grated zest and orange juice. Beat until blended and a smooth batter is formed. Turn into the tin and smooth the top.

Bake in the preheated oven for 35–45 minutes, or until golden and the sides begin to shrink from the edge of the tin. Cool before removing from the tin. Using a serrated knife, cut the cake horizontally about one third from the top and remove the top layer of the cake. If not using a ring mould tin, scoop out a centre ring of sponge from the top third and the bottom two thirds of the layer, making a hollow tunnel. Sprinkle the cut sides with the Cointreau.

For the filling, whip the cream and yogurt with the vanilla essence, Cointreau and icing sugar until soft peaks form. Chop the orange fruit and fold into the cream. Spoon some of this mixture on to the bottom cake layer. Transfer to a serving plate. Cover with the top layer of sponge and spread the remaining cream mixture over the top and sides. Press the chopped nuts into the sides of the cake and decorate the top with fruit. Dust the top with icing sugar.

Try this: FOR AN ALTERNATIVE: 262   FOR A COOKIE OR TRAYBAKE: 132

Italian Polenta Cake
with Mascarpone Cream

CUTS INTO 6–8 SLICES

1 tsp butter and flour for
   the tin
100 g/3½ oz plain flour
40 g/1½ oz polenta or
   yellow cornmeal
1 tsp baking powder
¼ tsp salt
grated zest of 1 lemon
2 large eggs

150 g/5 oz caster sugar
5 tbsp milk
½ tsp almond essence
2 tbsp raisins or sultanas
75 g/3 oz unsalted
   butter, softened
2 medium dessert pears,
   peeled, cored and
   thinly sliced

2 tbsp apricot jam
175 g/6 oz mascarpone cheese
1–2 tsp sugar
50 ml/2 fl oz double cream
2 tbsp Amaretto liqueur
   or rum
2–3 tbsp toasted flaked
   almonds
icing sugar, to dust

Preheat the oven to 190°C/375°F/Gas Mark 5, 10 minutes before baking. Butter a 23 cm/ 9 inch springform tin. Dust lightly with flour.

Stir the flour, polenta or cornmeal, baking powder, salt and lemon zest together. Beat the eggs and half the sugar until light and fluffy. Slowly beat in the milk and almond essence. Stir in the raisins or sultanas, then beat in the flour mixture and 50 g/2 oz of the butter. Spoon into the tin and smooth the top evenly. Arrange the pear slices on top in overlapping concentric circles.

Melt the remaining butter and brush over the pear slices. Sprinkle with the rest of the sugar. Bake in the preheated oven for about 40 minutes, until puffed and golden and the edges of the pears are lightly caramelised. Transfer to a wire rack. Reserve to cool in the tin for 15 minutes.

Remove the cake from the tin. Heat the apricot jam with 1 tablespoon of water and brush over the top of the cake to glaze. Beat the mascarpone cheese with the sugar to taste, the cream and Amaretto or rum until smooth and forming a soft dropping consistency. When cool, sprinkle the almonds over the polenta cake and dust with the icing sugar. Serve the cake with the liqueur-flavoured mascarpone cream.

Try this: FOR AN ALTERNATIVE: 222 FOR A COOKIE OR TRAYBAKE: 34

Lemony Coconut Cake

CUTS INTO 10-12 SLICES

275 g/10 oz plain flour
2 tbsp cornflour
1 tbsp baking powder
1 tsp salt
150 g/5 oz white vegetable
   fat or soft margarine
275 g/10 oz caster sugar
grated zest of 2 lemons

1 tsp vanilla essence
3 large eggs
150 ml/¼ pint milk
4 tbsp Malibu or rum
450 g/1 lb jar lemon curd
lime zest, to decorate

For the frosting:
275 g/10 oz caster sugar
125 ml/4 fl oz water
1 tbsp glucose
¼ tsp salt
1 tsp vanilla essence
3 large egg whites
75 g/3 oz shredded coconut

Preheat the oven to 180°C/350°F/Gas Mark 4, 10 minutes before baking. Lightly oil and flour two 20.5 cm/8 inch non-stick cake tins. Sift the flour, cornflour, baking powder and salt into a large bowl and add the white vegetable fat or margarine, sugar, lemon zest, vanilla essence, eggs and milk. With an electric whisk on a low speed, beat until blended, adding a little extra milk if the mixture is very stiff. Increase the speed to medium and beat for 2 minutes. Divide the mixture between the tins and smooth the tops. Bake in the preheated oven for 20–25 minutes, or until the cakes feel firm and are cooked. Cool before removing from the tins.

Put all the ingredients for the frosting, except the coconut, into a heatproof bowl placed over a saucepan of simmering water. Do not allow the base of the bowl to touch the water. Using an electric whisk, blend the frosting ingredients on a low speed. Increase the speed to high and beat for 7 minutes, until stiff and glossy. Remove the bowl from the heat and continue beating until cool. Cover with clingfilm.

Using a serrated knife, split the cake layers horizontally in half and sprinkle each cut surface with the Malibu or rum. Sandwich the cakes together with the lemon curd. Spread the top and sides generously with frosting. Sprinkle the coconut over the top of the cake and gently press on to the sides to cover. Decorate the coconut cake with the lime zest and serve.

Try this: FOR AN ALTERNATIVE: 188   FOR A COOKIE OR TRAYBAKE: 78

White Chocolate & Passion Fruit Cake

CUTS INTO 8-10 SLICES

125 g/4 oz white chocolate
125 g/4 oz butter
225 g/8 oz caster sugar
2 medium eggs
125 ml/4 fl oz soured cream
200 g/7 oz plain flour, sifted

75 g/3 oz self-raising
 flour, sifted
125 g/4 oz white chocolate,
 coarsely grated, to decorate

For the icing:
200 g/7 oz caster sugar
4 tbsp passion fruit juice
 (about 8–10 fruits, sieved)
1½ tbsp passion fruit seeds
250 g/9 oz unsalted butter

Preheat the oven to 180°C/350°F/Gas Mark 4, 10 minutes before baking. Lightly oil and line two 20.5 cm/8 inch cake tins. Melt the white chocolate in a heatproof bowl set over a saucepan of simmering water. Stir in 125 ml/4 fl oz warm water and stir, then leave to cool. Whisk the butter and sugar together until light and fluffy, add the eggs, one at a time, beating well after each addition. Beat in the chocolate mixture, soured cream and sifted flours. Divide the mixture into eight portions. Spread one portion into each of the tins. Bake in the preheated oven for 10 minutes, or until firm, then turn out onto wire racks. Repeat with the remaining mixture to make eight cake layers.

To make the icing, place 125 ml/4 fl oz of water with 50 g/2 oz of the sugar in a saucepan. Heat gently, stirring, until the sugar has dissolved. Bring to the boil and simmer for 2 minutes. Remove from the heat and cool, then add 2 tablespoons of the passion fruit juice. Reserve. Blend the remaining sugar with 50 ml/2 fl oz of water in a small saucepan and stir constantly over a low heat, without boiling, until the sugar has dissolved. Remove from the heat and cool. Stir in the remaining passion fruit juice and the seeds. Cool, then strain. Using an electric whisk, beat the butter in a bowl until very pale. Gradually beat in the syrup.

Place one layer of cake on a serving plate. Brush with the syrup and spread with a thin layer of icing. Repeat with the remaining cake, syrup and icing. Cover the cake with the remaining icing. Press the chocolate curls into the top and sides to decorate and serve.

 Try this: FOR AN ALTERNATIVE: 192   FOR A COOKIE OR TRAYBAKE: 134

Cranberry & White Chocolate Cake

SERVES 4

225 g/8 oz butter, softened
250 g/9 oz full fat soft cheese
150 g/5 oz light soft
 brown sugar
200 g/7 oz caster sugar

grated zest of ½ orange
1 tsp vanilla essence
4 medium eggs
375 g/13 oz plain flour
2 tsp baking powder

200 g/7 oz cranberries,
 thawed if frozen
225 g/8 oz white chocolate,
 coarsely chopped
2 tbsp orange juice

Preheat the oven to 180°C/350°F/Gas Mark 4, 10 minutes before baking. Lightly oil and flour a 23 cm/9 inch kugelhopf tin or ring tin.

Using an electric mixer, cream the butter and cheese with the sugars until light and fluffy. Add the grated orange zest and vanilla essence and beat until smooth, then beat in the eggs, one at a time.

Sift the flour and baking powder together and stir into the creamed mixture, beating well after each addition. Fold in the cranberries and 175 g/6 oz of the white chocolate. Spoon into the prepared tin and bake in the preheated oven for 1 hour, or until firm and a skewer inserted into the centre comes out clean. Cool in the tin before turning out onto on a wire rack.

Melt the remaining white chocolate, stir until smooth, then stir in the orange juice and leave to cool until thickened. Transfer the cake to a serving plate and spoon over the white chocolate and orange glaze. Leave to set.

Try this: FOR AN ALTERNATIVE: 296 FOR A COOKIE OR TRAYBAKE: 140

Almond Angel Cake with Amaretto Cream

CUTS INTO 10-12 SLICES

175 g/6 oz icing sugar, plus 2–3 tbsp
150 g/5 oz plain flour
350 ml/12 fl oz egg whites (about 10 large egg whites)

1½ tsp cream of tartar
½ tsp vanilla essence
1 tsp almond essence
¼ tsp salt
200 g/7 oz caster sugar

175 ml/6 fl oz double cream
2 tablespoons Amaretto liqueur
fresh raspberries, to decorate

Preheat the oven to 180°C/350°F/Gas Mark 4, 10 minutes before baking. Sift together the 175 g/6 oz icing sugar and flour. Stir to blend, then sift again and reserve. Using an electric whisk, beat the egg whites, cream of tartar, vanilla essence, ½ teaspoon of almond essence and salt on medium speed until soft peaks form. Gradually add the caster sugar, 2 tablespoons at a time, beating well after each addition, until stiff peaks form.

Sift about one third of the flour mixture over the egg white mixture and using a metal spoon or rubber spatula, gently fold into the egg white mixture. Repeat, folding the flour mixture into the egg white mixture in two more batches. Spoon gently into an ungreased angel food cake tin or 25.5 cm/10 inch tube tin.

Bake in the preheated oven until risen and golden on top and the surface springs back quickly when gently pressed with a clean finger. Immediately invert the cake tin and cool completely in the tin. When cool, carefully run a sharp knife around the edge of the tin and the centre ring to loosen the cake from the edge. Ease the cake from the tin and invert on to a cake plate. Thickly dust the cake with the extra icing sugar.

Whip the cream with the remaining almond essence, Amaretto liqueur and a little more icing sugar, until soft peaks form. Fill a piping bag fitted with a star nozzle with half the cream and pipe around the bottom edge of the cake. Decorate the edge with the fresh raspberries and serve the remaining cream separately.

Try this: FOR AN ALTERNATIVE: 204   FOR A COOKIE OR TRAYBAKE: 60

Whole Orange & Chocolate Cake With Marmalade Cream

CUTS 6-8 SLICES

1 small orange, scrubbed
2 medium eggs, separated,
   plus 1 whole egg
150 g/5 oz caster sugar
125 g/4 oz ground almonds

75 g/3 oz plain dark
   chocolate, melted
100 ml/3½ fl oz
   double cream
200 g/7 oz full fat soft cheese

25 g/1 oz icing sugar
2 tbsp orange marmalade
orange zest, to decorate

Preheat the oven to 180°C/350°F/Gas Mark 4, 10 minutes before baking. Lightly oil and line the base of a 900 g/2 lb loaf tin. Place the orange in a small saucepan, cover with cold water and bring to the boil. Simmer for 1 hour until completely soft. Drain and leave to cool.

Place 2 egg yolks, 1 whole egg and the sugar in a heatproof bowl set over a saucepan of simmering water and whisk until doubled in bulk. Remove from the heat and continue to whisk for 5 minutes until cooled. Cut the whole orange in half and discard the seeds, then place into a food processor or blender and blend to a purée. Carefully fold the purée into the egg yolk mixture with the ground almonds and melted chocolate. Whisk the egg whites until stiff peaks form. Fold a large spoonful of the egg whites into the chocolate mixture, then gently fold the remaining egg whites into the mixture.

Pour into the prepared tin and bake in the preheated oven for 50 minutes, or until firm and a skewer inserted into the centre comes out clean. Cool in the tin before turning out of the tin and carefully discarding the lining paper.

Meanwhile, whip the double cream until just thickened. In another bowl, blend the soft cheese with the icing sugar and marmalade until smooth, then fold in the double cream. Chill the marmalade cream in the refrigerator until required. Decorate with orange zest and serve the cake cut in slices with the marmalade cream.

Try this: FOR AN ALTERNATIVE: 216   FOR A COOKIE OR TRAYBAKE: 82

Toffee Walnut Swiss Roll

CUTS INTO 10-12 SLICES

4 large eggs, separated
½ tsp cream of tartar
125 g/4 oz icing sugar, plus
   extra to dust
½ tsp vanilla essence
125 g/4 oz self-raising flour

**For the toffee
  walnut filling:**
2 tbsp plain flour
150 ml/¼ pint milk
5 tbsp golden syrup or
  maple syrup

2 large egg yolks, beaten
100 g/3½ oz walnuts
  or pecans, toasted
  and chopped
300 ml/½ pint double
  cream, whipped

Preheat the oven to 190°C/375°F/Gas Mark 5, 10 minutes before baking. Lightly oil and line a Swiss roll tin with non-stick baking paper. Beat the egg whites and cream of tartar until softly peaking. Gradually beat in 50 g/2 oz of the icing sugar until stiff peaks form. In another bowl, beat the egg yolks with the remaining icing sugar until thick. Beat in the vanilla essence. Gently fold in the flour and egg whites alternately using a metal spoon or rubber spatula.

Spoon the batter into the tin and spread evenly. Bake in the preheated oven for 12 minutes, or until well risen and golden and the cake springs back when pressed with a clean finger. Lay a clean tea towel on a work surface and lay a piece of baking paper about 33 cm/13 inches long on the towel and dust with icing sugar. As soon as the cake is cooked turn out on to the paper. Peel off the lining paper and cut off the crisp edges of the cake. Starting at one narrow end, roll the cake with the paper and towel. Transfer to a wire rack and cool completely.

For the filling, put the flour, milk and syrup into a small saucepan and place over a gentle heat. Bring to the boil, whisking until thick and smooth. Remove from the heat and slowly beat into the beaten egg yolks. Pour the mixture back into the saucepan and cook over a low heat until it thickens and coats the back of a spoon. Strain the mixture into a bowl and stir in the chopped walnuts or pecans. Cool, stirring occasionally, then fold in about half of the whipped cream. Unroll the cooled cake and spread the filling over the cake. Re-roll and decorate with the remaining cream. Sprinkle with the icing sugar and serve.

Try this: FOR AN ALTERNATIVE: 200 FOR A COOKIE OR TRAYBAKE: 120

Coffee & Walnut Gateau with Brandied Prunes

CUTS INTO 10-12 SLICES

For the prunes:
225 g/8 oz ready-to-eat pitted dried prunes
150 ml/¼ pint cold tea
3 tbsp brandy

For the cake:
450 g/1 lb walnut pieces

50 g/2 oz self-raising flour
½ tsp baking powder
1 tsp instant coffee powder (not granules)
5 large eggs, separated
¼ tsp cream of tartar
150 g/5 oz caster sugar
2 tbsp sunflower oil

8 walnut halves, to decorate

For the filling:
600 ml/1 pint double cream
4 tbsp icing sugar, sifted
2 tbsp coffee-flavoured liqueur

Preheat the oven to 180°C/350°F/Gas Mark 4, 10 minutes before baking. Put the prunes in a small bowl with the tea and brandy and allow to stand for 3–4 hours or overnight. Oil and line the bases of two 23 cm/9 inch cake tins. Chop the walnut pieces in a food processor and reserve a quarter of them. Add the flour, baking powder and coffee and blend until finely ground.

Whisk the egg whites with the cream of tartar until soft peaks form. Sprinkle in one-third of the sugar, 2 tablespoons at a time, until stiff peaks form. In another bowl, beat the egg yolks, oil and the remaining sugar, until thick. Using a metal spoon or rubber spatula, alternately fold in the nut mixture and egg whites until just blended. Divide the mixture evenly between the tins, smoothing the tops. Bake in the preheated oven for 30–35 minutes, or until the top of the cakes spring back when lightly pressed. When cool, remove from the tins.

Drain the prunes, reserving the soaking liquid. Dry on kitchen paper, then chop and reserve. Whisk the cream with the icing sugar and liqueur until soft peaks form. Spoon one-eighth of the cream into a pastry bag fitted with a star nozzle. Cut the cake layers in half horizontally. Sprinkle each cut side with 1 tablespoon of the prune-soaking liquid. Sandwich the cakes together with half the cream and all the chopped prunes. Spread the remaining cream around the sides of the cake and press in the reserved chopped walnuts. Pipe rosettes around the edge of the cake and serve.

Try this: FOR AN ALTERNATIVE: 262   FOR A COOKIE OR TRAYBAKE: 30

Black & White Torte

CUTS INTO 8-10 SLICES

4 medium eggs
150 g/5 oz caster sugar
50 g/2 oz cornflour
50 g/2 oz plain flour
50 g/2 oz self-raising flour

900 ml/1½ pints double cream
150 g/5 oz plain dark
   chocolate, chopped
300 g/11 oz white
   chocolate, chopped

6 tbsp Grand Marnier, or
   other orange liqueur
cocoa powder for dusting

Preheat the oven to 180°C/350°F/Gas Mark 4, 10 minutes before baking. Line a 23 cm/ 9 inch round cake tin. Beat the eggs and sugar in a large bowl until thick and creamy. Sift together the cornflour, plain flour and self-raising flour three times, then lightly fold into the egg mixture. Spoon the mixture into the prepared tin and bake in the preheated oven for 35–40 minutes or until firm. Turn the cake out onto a wire rack and leave to cool.

Place 300 ml/½ pint of the double cream in a saucepan and bring to the boil. Immediately remove from the heat and add the plain chocolate and a further tablespoon of the liqueur. Stir until smooth. Repeat using the remaining cream, white chocolate and liqueur. Chill in the refrigerator for 2 hours, then whisk each mixture until thick and creamy.

Place the dark chocolate mixture in a piping bag fitted with a plain nozzle and place half the white chocolate mixture in a separate piping bag fitted with a plain nozzle. Reserve the remaining white chocolate mixture.

Split the cold cake horizontally into two layers. Brush or drizzle the remaining liqueur over the cakes. Put one layer onto a serving plate. Pipe alternating rings of white and dark chocolate mixture to cover the first layer of cake. Use the reserved white chocolate mixture to cover the top and sides of the cake. Dust with cocoa powder, cut into slices and serve. Store in the refrigerator.

Try this: FOR AN ALTERNATIVE: 282   FOR A COOKIE OR TRAYBAKE: 76

Dark Chocolate Layered Torte

CUTS INTO 10-12 SLICES

175 g/6 oz butter
1 tbsp instant coffee granules
150 g/ 5 oz plain
   dark chocolate
350 g/12 oz caster sugar
150 g/5 oz self-raising flour

125 g/4 oz plain flour
2 tbsp cocoa powder
2 medium eggs
1 tsp vanilla essence
215 g/7½ oz plain dark
   chocolate, melted

125 g/4 oz butter, melted
40 g/1½ oz icing sugar, sifted
2 tsp raspberry jam
2½ tbsp chocolate liqueur
100 g/3½ oz toasted
   flaked almonds

Preheat the oven to 150°C/300°F/Gas Mark 2, 10 minutes before baking. Line a 23 cm/9 inch square cake tin. Melt the butter in a saucepan, remove from the heat and stir in the coffee granules and 225 ml/8 fl oz hot water. Add the plain dark chocolate and sugar and stir until smooth, then pour into a bowl. In another bowl, sift together the flours and cocoa powder. Using an electric whisk, whisk the sifted mixture into the chocolate mixture until smooth. Beat in the eggs and vanilla essence. Pour into the tin and bake in the preheated oven for 1¼ hours or until firm. Leave for at least 5 minutes before turning out onto a wire rack to cool.

Meanwhile, mix together 200 g/7 oz of the melted dark chocolate with the butter and icing sugar and beat until smooth. Leave to cool, then beat again. Reserve 4–5 tablespoons of the chocolate filling. Cut the cooled cake in half to make two rectangles, then split each rectangle in three horizontally. Place one cake layer on a serving plate and spread thinly with the jam, then a thin layer of dark chocolate filling. Top with a second cake layer and sprinkle with a little liqueur, then spread thinly with filling. Repeat with the remaining cake layers, liqueur and filling.

Chill in the refrigerator for 2–3 hours or until firm. Cover the cake with the reserved chocolate filling and press the flaked almonds into the sides of the cake. Place the remaining melted chocolate in a non-stick baking parchment piping bag. Snip a small hole in the tip and pipe thin lines 2 cm/¾ inch apart crossways over the cake. Drag a cocktail stick lengthways through the icing in alternating directions to create a feathered effect on the top. Serve.

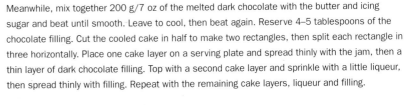

Try this: FOR AN ALTERNATIVE: 272   FOR A COOKIE OR TRAYBAKE: 86

French Chocolate Pecan Torte

CUTS INTO 16 SLICES

200 g/7 oz plain dark
  chocolate, chopped
150 g/5 oz butter, diced
4 large eggs
100 g/3½ oz caster sugar
2 tsp vanilla essence

125 g/4 oz pecans,
  finely ground
2 tsp ground cinnamon
24 pecan halves,
  lightly toasted,
  to decorate

For the chocolate glaze:
125 g/4 oz plain dark
  chocolate, chopped
60 g/2½ oz butter, diced
2 tbsp clear honey
¼ tsp ground cinnamon

Preheat the oven to 180°C/350°F/Gas Mark 4, 10 minutes before baking. Lightly butter and line a 20.5 x 5 cm/8 x 2 inch springform tin with non-stick baking paper. Wrap the tin in a large sheet of tinfoil to prevent water seeping in.

Melt the chocolate and butter in a saucepan over a low heat and stir until smooth. Remove from the heat and cool. Using an electric whisk, beat the eggs, sugar and vanilla essence until light and foamy. Gradually beat in the melted chocolate, ground nuts and cinnamon, then pour into the prepared tin.

Set the foil-wrapped tin in a large roasting tin and pour in enough boiling water to come 2 cm/¾ inches up the sides of the tin. Bake in the preheated oven until the edge is set, but the centre is still soft when the tin is gently shaken. Remove from the oven and place on a wire rack to cool.

For the glaze, melt all the ingredients over a low heat until melted and smooth, then remove from the heat. Dip each pecan halfway into the glaze and set on a sheet of non-stick baking paper until set. Allow the remaining glaze to thicken slightly. Remove the cake from the tin and invert. Pour the glaze over the cake smoothing the top and spreading the glaze around the sides. Arrange the glazed pecans around the edge of the torte. Allow to set and serve.

Sachertorte

CUTS INTO 10-12 SLICES

150 g/5 oz plain
  dark chocolate
150 g/5 oz unsalted
  butter, softened
125 g/4 oz caster sugar,

plus 2 tbsp
3 medium eggs, separated
150 g/5 oz plain flour, sifted
To decorate:
225 g/8 oz apricot jam

125 g/4 oz plain dark
  chocolate, chopped
125 g/4 oz unsalted butter
25 g/1 oz milk chocolate

Preheat the oven to 180°C/350°F/Gas Mark 4, 10 minutes before baking. Lightly oil and line a deep 23 cm/9 inch cake tin. Melt the 150 g/5 oz of chocolate in a heatproof bowl set over a saucepan of simmering water. Stir in 1 tablespoon of water and leave to cool. Beat the butter and 125 g/4 oz of the sugar together until light and fluffy. Beat in the egg yolks, one at a time, beating well between each addition. Stir in the melted chocolate, then the flour.

In a clean, grease-free bowl, whisk the egg whites until stiff peaks form, then whisk in the remaining sugar. Fold into the chocolate mixture and spoon into the prepared tin. Bake in the pre-heated oven for 30 minutes until firm. Leave for 5 minutes, then turn out onto a wire rack to cool. Leave the cake upside down.

To decorate the cake, split the cold cake in two and place one half on a serving plate. Heat the jam and rub through a fine sieve. Brush half the jam onto the first cake half, then cover with the remaining cake layer and brush with the remaining jam. Leave at room temperature for 1 hour or until the jam has set.

Place the plain dark chocolate with the butter into a heatproof bowl set over a saucepan of simmering water and heat until the chocolate has melted. Stir occasionally until smooth, then leave until thickened. Use to cover the cake. Melt the milk chocolate in a heatproof bowl set over a saucepan of simmering water. Place in a small greaseproof piping bag and snip a small hole at the tip. Pipe 'Sache'r with a large 'S' on the top. Leave to set at room temperature.

Try this: FOR AN ALTERNATIVE: 228   FOR A COOKIE OR TRAYBAKE: 96

Mocha Truffle Cake

CUTS INTO 8-10 SLICES

3 medium eggs
125 g/4 oz caster sugar
40 g/1½ oz cornflour
40 g/1½ oz self-raising flour
2 tbsp cocoa powder

2 tbsp milk
2 tbsp coffee liqueur
100 g/3½ oz white chocolate,
  melted and cooled
200 g/7 oz plain dark

chocolate, melted
  and cooled
600 ml/1 pint double cream
200 g/7 oz milk chocolate
100 g/3½ oz unsalted butter

Preheat the oven to 180°C/350°F/Gas Mark 4, 10 minutes before cooking. Lightly oil and line a deep 23 cm/9 inch round cake tin.

Beat the eggs and sugar in a bowl until thick and creamy. Sift together the cornflour, self-raising flour and cocoa powder and fold lightly into the egg mixture. Spoon into the prepared tin and bake in the preheated oven for 30 minutes or until firm. Turn out onto a wire rack and leave until cold. Split the cold cake horizontally into two layers. Mix together the milk and coffee liqueur and brush onto the cake layers.

Stir the cooled white chocolate into one bowl and the cooled plain dark chocolate into another one. Whip the cream until soft peaks form, then divide between the two bowls and stir. Place one layer of cake in a 23 cm/9 inch springform tin. Spread with half the white chocolate cream. Top with the dark chocolate cream, then the remaining white chocolate cream, then place the remaining cake layer on top. Chill in the refrigerator for 4 hours or overnight until set.

When ready to serve, melt the milk chocolate and butter in a heatproof bowl set over a saucepan of simmering water and stir until smooth. Remove from the heat and leave until thick enough to spread, then use to cover the top and sides of the cake. Leave to set at room temperature, then chill in the refrigerator. Cut the cake into slices and serve.

Try this: FOR AN ALTERNATIVE: 266   FOR A COOKIE OR TRAYBAKE: 42

Chocolate Chiffon Cake

CUTS INTO 10-12 SLICES

50 g/2 oz cocoa powder
300 g/11 oz self-raising flour
550 g/1¼ lb caster sugar
7 medium eggs, separated
125 ml/4 fl oz vegetable oil
1 tsp vanilla essence

75 g/3 oz walnuts
50 g/2 oz plain dark
   chocolate
200 g/7 oz plain dark
   chocolate, melted

For the icing:
175 g/6 oz butter
275 g/10 oz icing sugar, sifted
2 tbsp cocoa powder, sifted
2 tbsp brandy

Preheat the oven to 170°C/325°F/Gas Mark 3, 10 minutes before serving. Line a 23 cm/
9 inch round cake tin. Lightly oil a baking sheet. Blend the cocoa powder with 175 ml/6 fl oz
boiling water and leave to cool. Place the flour and 350 g/12 oz of the caster sugar in a large
bowl, and add the cocoa mixture, egg yolks, oil and vanilla essence. Whisk until smooth and
lighter in colour. Whisk the egg whites in a clean, grease-free bowl until soft peaks form, then
fold into the cocoa mixture. Pour into the prepared tin and bake in the preheated oven for 1
hour or until firm. Leave for 5 minutes before turning out onto a wire rack to cool.

To make the icing, cream together 125 g/4 oz of the butter with the icing sugar, cocoa powder
and brandy until smooth, then reserve. Melt the remaining butter and blend with 150 g/5 oz of
the melted dark chocolate. Stir until smooth and then leave until thickened. Place the
remaining caster sugar into a heavy-based saucepan over a low heat and heat until the sugar
has melted and is a deep golden brown. Add the walnuts and the remaining melted chocolate
to the melted sugar and pour onto the prepared baking sheet. Leave until cold and brittle, then
chop finely. Reserve.

Split the cake into three layers, place one layer onto a serving plate and spread with half of
the brandy butter icing. Top with a second cake layer and spread with the remaining brandy
butter icing. Arrange the third cake layer on top. Cover the cake with the thickened chocolate
glaze. Sprinkle with the walnut praline and serve.

Try this: FOR AN ALTERNATIVE: 268   FOR A COOKIE OR TRAYBAKE: 38

Chocolate Box Cake

CUTS INTO 16 SLICES

For the chocolate sponge:
175 g/6 oz self-raising flour
1 tsp baking powder
175 g/6 oz caster sugar
175 g/6 oz butter, softened
3 large eggs
25 g/1 oz cocoa powder

150 g/5 oz apricot preserve
cocoa powder, to dust

For the chocolate box:
275 g/10 oz plain dark
  chocolate

For the chocolate topping:
450 ml ¾ pint double cream
275 g/10 oz plain dark
  chocolate, melted
2 tbsp brandy
1 tsp cocoa powder,
  to decorate

Preheat the oven to 180°C/350°F/Gas Mark 4, 10 minutes before baking. Lightly oil and flour a 20.5 cm/8 inch square cake tin. Sift the flour and baking powder into a large bowl and stir in the sugar. Using an electric whisk, beat in the butter and eggs. Blend the cocoa powder with 1 tablespoon of water, then beat into the creamed mixture. Turn into the tin and bake in the preheated oven for about 25 minutes, or until well risen and cooked. Remove and cool before removing the cake from the tin.

To make the chocolate box, break the chocolate into small pieces, place in a heatproof bowl over a saucepan of gently simmering water and leave until soft. Stir it occasionally until melted and smooth. Line a Swiss roll tin with non-stick baking paper then pour in the melted chocolate, tilting the tin to level. Leave until set. Once the chocolate is set, turn out on to a chopping board and carefully strip off the paper. Cut into four strips, the same length as the cooked sponge, using a large sharp knife that has been dipped into hot water. Gently heat the apricot preserve and sieve to remove lumps. Brush over the top and sides of the cake. Carefully place the chocolate strips around the cake sides and press lightly. Leave to set for at least 10 minutes.

For the topping, whisk the cream to soft peaks and quickly fold into the melted chocolate with the brandy. Spoon the chocolate whipped cream into a pastry bag fitted with a star nozzle and pipe a decorative design over the surface. Dust with cocoa power and serve.

Try this: FOR AN ALTERNATIVE: 280   FOR A COOKIE OR TRAYBAKE: 90

Rich Devil's Food Cake

450 g/1 lb plain flour	brown sugar	½ tsp salt
1 tbsp bicarbonate of soda	2 tsp vanilla essence	125 g/4 oz plain dark
½ tsp salt	4 large eggs	chocolate, chopped
75 g/3 oz cocoa powder		225 ml/8 fl oz milk
300 ml/½ pint milk	**For the chocolate**	2 tbsp golden syrup
150 g/5 oz butter, softened	**fudge frosting:**	125 g/4 oz butter, diced
400 g/14 oz soft dark	275 g/10 oz caster sugar	2 tsp vanilla essence

Preheat the oven to 180°C/350°F/Gas Mark 4, 10 minutes before baking. Lightly oil and line the bases of three 23 cm/9 inch cake tins with greaseproof paper. Sift the flour, bicarbonate of soda and salt into a bowl. Sift the cocoa powder into another bowl and gradually whisk in a little of the milk to form a paste. Continue whisking in the milk until a smooth mixture results.

Beat the butter, sugar and vanilla essence until light and fluffy then gradually beat in the eggs, beating well after each addition. Stir in the flour and cocoa mixtures alternately in three or four batches. Divide the mixture evenly among the three tins, smoothing the surfaces evenly. Bake in the preheated oven for 25–35 minutes, until cooked and firm to the touch. Remove, cool and turn out on to a wire rack. Discard the lining paper.

To make the frosting, put the sugar, salt and chocolate in a heavy-based saucepan and stir in the milk until blended. Add the golden syrup and butter. Bring the mixture to the boil over a medium-high heat, stirring to help dissolve the sugar. Boil for 1 minute, stirring constantly. Remove from the heat, stir in the vanilla essence and cool. When cool, whisk until thickened and slightly lightened in colour. Sandwich the three cake layers together with about a third of the frosting, placing the third cake layer with the flat side up. Transfer the cake to a serving plate and, using a metal palette knife, spread the remaining frosting over the top and sides. Swirl the top to create a decorative effect and serve.

Try this: FOR AN ALTERNATIVE: 278 FOR A COOKIE OR TRAYBAKE: 94

Double Marble Cake

CUTS INTO 8-10 SLICES

75 g/3 oz white chocolate
75 g/3 oz plain
　　dark chocolate
175 g/6 oz caster sugar
175 g/6 oz butter
4 medium eggs, separated

125 g/4 oz plain flour, sifted
75 g/3 oz ground almonds

Fot the topping:
50 g/2 oz white chocolate,
　　chopped

75 g/3 oz plain dark
　　chocolate, chopped
50 ml/2 fl oz double cream
100 g/3½ oz unsalted butter

Preheat the oven to 180°C/350°F/Gas Mark 4, 10 minutes before baking. Lightly oil and line the base of a 20.5 cm/8 inch cake tin. Break the white and dark chocolate into small pieces, then place in two separate bowls placed over two pans of simmering water, ensuring that the bowls are not touching the water. Heat the chocolate until melted and smooth.

In a large bowl, cream the sugar and butter together until light and fluffy. Beat in the egg yolks, one at a time and add a spoonful of flour after each addition. Stir in the ground almonds. In another bowl whisk the egg whites until stiff. Gently fold in the egg whites and the remaining sifted flour alternately into the almond mixture until all the flour and egg whites have been incorporated. Divide the mixture between two bowls. Gently stir the white chocolate into one bowl, then add the dark chocolate to the other bowl.

Place alternating spoonfuls of the chocolate mixtures in the prepared cake tin. Using a skewer, swirl the mixtures together to get a marbled effect, then tap the tin on the work surface to level the mixture. Bake in the preheated oven for 40 minutes, or until cooked through, then leave to cool for 5 minutes in the tin, before turning out onto a wire rack to cool completely.

Melt the chocolate with the cream and butter and stir until smooth. Cool, then whisk until thick and swirl over the top of the cake.

Chocolate Buttermilk Cake

CUTS INTO 8-10 SLICES

175 g/6 oz butter
1 tsp vanilla essence
350 g/12 oz caster sugar
4 medium eggs, separated

100 g/3½ oz self-raising flour
40 g/1½ oz cocoa powder
175 ml/6 fl oz buttermilk
200 g/7 oz plain

dark chocolate
100 g/3½ oz butter
300 ml/½ pint double cream

Preheat the oven to 180°C/350°F/Gas Mark 4, 10 minutes before baking. Lightly oil and line a deep 23 cm/9 inch round cake tin. Cream together the butter, vanilla essence and sugar until light and fluffy, then beat in the egg yolks, one at a time.

Sift together the flour and cocoa powder and fold into the egg mixture together with the buttermilk. Whisk the egg whites until soft peaks form and fold carefully into the chocolate mixture in two batches. Spoon the mixture into the prepared tin and bake in the preheated oven for 1 hour or until firm. Cool slightly, then turn out onto a wire rack and leave until completely cold.

Place the chocolate and butter together in a heatproof bowl set over a saucepan of simmering water and heat until melted. Stir until smooth, then leave at room temperature until the chocolate is thick enough to spread.

Split the cake horizontally in half. Use some of the chocolate mixture to sandwich the two halves together. Spread and decorate the top of the cake with the remaining chocolate mixture. Finally, whip the cream until soft peaks form and use to spread around the sides of the cake. Chill in the refrigerator until required. Serve cut into slices. Store in the refrigerator.

Try this: FOR AN ALTERNATIVE: 278   FOR A COOKIE OR TRAYBAKE: 80

Chocolate Mousse Sponge

CUTS INTO 8-10 SLICES

3 medium eggs
75 g/3 oz caster sugar
1 tsp vanilla essence
50 g/2 oz self-raising
    flour, sifted
25 g/1 oz ground almonds
50 g/2 oz plain dark

chocolate, grated
icing sugar, for dusting
freshly sliced strawberries,
    to decorate

For the mousse:
2 sheets gelatine

50 ml/2 fl oz double cream
100 g/3½ oz plain dark
    chocolate, chopped
1 tsp vanilla essence
4 medium egg whites
125 g/4 oz caster sugar

Preheat the oven to 180°C/350°F/Gas Mark 4, 10 minutes before baking. Lightly oil and line a 23 cm/9 inch round cake tin and lightly oil the sides of a 23 cm/9 inch springform tin. Whisk the eggs, sugar and vanilla essence until thick and creamy. Fold in the flour, ground almonds and dark chocolate. Spoon the mixture into the prepared round cake tin and bake in the preheated oven for 25 minutes or until firm. Turn out onto a wire rack to cool.

For the mousse, soak the gelatine in 50 ml/2 fl oz of cold water for 5 minutes until softened. Meanwhile, heat the double cream in a small saucepan, when almost boiling, remove from the heat and stir in the chocolate and vanilla essence. Stir until the chocolate melts. Squeeze the excess water out of the gelatine and add to the chocolate mixture. Stir until dissolved, then pour into a large bowl. Whisk the egg whites until stiff, then gradually add the caster sugar, whisking well between each addition. Fold the egg white mixture into the chocolate mixture in two batches.

Split the cake into two layers. Place one layer in the bottom of the springform tin. Pour in the chocolate mousse mixture, then top with the second layer of cake. Chill in the refrigerator for 4 hours or until the mousse has set. Loosen the sides and remove the cake from the tin. Dust with icing sugar and decorate the top with a few freshly sliced strawberries. Serve cut into slices.

Try this: FOR AN ALTERNATIVE: 288 FOR A COOKIE OR TRAYBAKE: 112

Chocolate Mousse Cake

CUTS INTO 8-10 SERVINGS

For the cake:
450 g/1 lb plain dark
    chocolate, chopped
125 g/4 oz butter, softened
3 tbsp brandy
9 large eggs, separated

150 g/5 oz caster sugar

For the chocolate glaze:
225 ml/8 fl oz double cream
225 g/8 oz plain dark
    chocolate, chopped

2 tbsp brandy
1 tbsp single cream and
    white chocolate curls,
    to decorate

Preheat the oven to 180°C/350°F/Gas Mark 4, 10 minutes before baking. Line the bases of two 20.5 cm/8 inch springform tins with baking paper. Melt the chocolate and butter in a bowl set over a saucepan of simmering water. Stir until smooth. Remove from the heat and stir in the brandy. Whisk the egg yolks and the sugar, reserving 2 tablespoons of the sugar, until thick and creamy. Slowly beat in the chocolate mixture until smooth and well blended. Whisk the egg whites until soft peaks form, then sprinkle over the remaining sugar and continue whisking until stiff but not dry.

Fold a large spoonful of the egg whites into the chocolate mixture. Gently fold in the remaining egg whites. Divide about two thirds of the mixture evenly between the tins, tapping to distribute the mixture evenly. Reserve the remaining chocolate mousse mixture for the filling. Bake in the preheated oven for about 20 minutes, or until the cakes are well risen and set. Remove and cool for at least 1 hour. Loosen the edges of the cake layers with a knife. Using your fingertips, lightly press the crusty edges down. Pour the rest of the mousse over one layer, spreading until even. Unclip the side, remove the other cake from the tin and gently invert on to the mousse, bottom side up to make a flat top layer. Discard the lining paper and chill for 4–6 hours, or until set.

To make the glaze, melt the cream and chocolate with the brandy in a heavy-based saucepan and stir until smooth. Cool until thickened. Unclip the side of the mousse cake and place on a wire rack. Pour over half the glaze and spread to cover. Allow to set, then decorate with chocolate curls. To serve, heat the remaining glaze and pour round each slice, and dot with cream.

Try this: FOR AN ALTERNATIVE: 286   FOR A COOKIE OR TRAYBAKE: 136

Chocolate Roulade

CUTS INTO 8 SLICES

200 g/7 oz plain dark chocolate
200 g/7 oz caster sugar
7 medium eggs, separated
300 ml/½ pint double cream

3 tbsp Cointreau or
   Grand Marnier
4 tbsp icing sugar for dusting

To decorate:
fresh raspberries
sprigs of fresh mint

Preheat the oven to 180°C/350°F/Gas Mark 4, 10 minutes before baking. Lightly oil and line a 33 cm x 23 cm/13 inch x 9 inch Swiss roll tin with nonstick baking parchment. Break the chocolate into small pieces into a heatproof bowl set over a saucepan of simmering water. Leave until almost melted, stirring occasionally. Remove from the heat and leave to stand for 5 minutes.

Whisk the egg yolks with the sugar until pale and creamy and the whisk leaves a trail in the mixture when lifted, then carefully fold in the melted chocolate.

In a clean grease-free bowl, whisk the egg whites until stiff, then fold 1 large spoonful into the chocolate mixture. Mix lightly, then gently fold in the remaining egg whites. Pour the mixture into the prepared tin and level the surface. Bake in the oven for 20–25 minutes or until firm.

Remove the cake from the oven, leave in the tin and cover with a wire rack and a damp tea towel. Leave for 8 hours or preferably overnight.

Dust a large sheet of nonstick baking parchment generously with 2 tablespoons of the icing sugar. Unwrap the cake and turn out onto the greaseproof paper. Remove the baking parchment. Whip the cream with the liqueur until soft peaks form. Spread over the cake, leaving a 2.5 cm /1 inch border all round.

Using the paper to help, roll the cake up from a short end. Transfer to a serving plate, seam-side down, and dust with the remaining icing sugar. Decorate with fresh raspberries and mint. Serve.

Try this: FOR AN ALTERNATIVE: 292 FOR A COOKIE OR TRAYBAKE: 86

Chocolate Roulade
with Toasted Coconut

SERVES 8

	For the filling:	coconut, chilled
150 g/5 oz golden	300 ml/½ pint double cream	2 tbsp icing sugar
caster sugar	3 tbsp whisky	coarsely shredded
5 medium eggs, separated	50 g/2 oz creamed	coconut, toasted
50 g/2 oz cocoa powder		

Preheat the oven to 180°C/350°F/Gas Mark 4, 10 minutes before baking. Oil and line a 33 x 23 cm/13 x 9 inch Swiss roll tin with a single sheet of non-stick baking parchment. Dust a large sheet of baking parchment with 2 tablespoons if the caster sugar.

Place the egg yolks in a bowl with the remaining sugar, set over a saucepan of gently simmering water and whisk until pale and thick. Sift the cocoa powder into the mixture and carefully fold in.

Whisk the egg whites in a clean, grease-free bowl until soft peaks form. Gently add 1 tablespoon of the whisked egg whites into the chocolate mixture then fold in the remaining whites. Spoon the mixture onto the prepared tin, smoothing the mixture into the corners. Bake in the preheated oven for 20–25 minutes, or until risen and springy to the touch.

Turn the cooked roulade out onto the sugar-dusted baking parchment and carefully peel off the lining paper. Cover with a clean damp tea towel and leave to cool.

To make the filling, pour the cream and whisky into a bowl and whisk until the cream holds its shape. Grate in the chilled creamed coconut, add the icing sugar and gently stir in. Uncover the roulade and spoon about three quarters of coconut cream on the roulade and roll up. Spoon the remaining cream on the top and sprinkle with the coconut, then serve.

Try this: FOR AN ALTERNATIVE: 290 FOR A COOKIE OR TRAYBAKE: 128

Grated Chocolate Roulade

CUTS 8 SLICES

4 medium eggs, separated	75 g/3 oz self-raising	150 ml/¼ pint double cream
125 g/4 oz caster sugar	flour, sifted	2 tsp icing sugar
60 g/2½ oz plain dark	2 tbsp caster sugar, plus	1 tsp vanilla essence
chocolate, grated	extra for sprinkling	chocolate curls, to decorate

Preheat the oven to 180°C/350°F/Gas Mark 4, 10 minutes before serving. Lightly oil and line a 20.5 x 30.5 cm/8 x 12 inch Swiss roll tin. Beat the egg yolks and sugar with an electric mixer for 5 minutes or until thick, then stir in 2 tablespoons of hot water and the grated chocolate. Finally fold in the sifted flour.

Whisk the egg whites until stiff, then fold 1–2 tablespoons of egg white into the chocolate mixture. Mix lightly, then gently fold in the remaining egg white. Pour into the prepared tin and bake in the preheated oven for about 12 minutes or until firm.

Place a large sheet of non-stick baking parchment on to a work surface and sprinkle liberally with caster sugar. Turn the cake onto the baking parchment, discard the lining paper and trim away the crisp edges. Roll up as for a Swiss roll cake, leave for 2 minutes, then unroll and leave to cool.

Beat the double cream with the icing sugar and vanilla essence until thick. Reserve a little for decoration, then spread the remaining cream over the cake, leaving a 2.5 cm/1 inch border all round. Using the greaseproof paper, roll up from a short end.

Carefully transfer the roulade to a large serving plate and use the reserved cream to decorate the top. Add the chocolate curls just before serving, then cut into slices and serve. Store in the refrigerator

Try this: FOR AN ALTERNATIVE: 296   FOR A COOKIE OR TRAYBAKE: 36

Christmas Cranberry Chocolate Roulade

CUTS INTO 12-14 SLICES

For the granache frosting:
300 ml/½ pint double cream
350 g/12 oz plain dark
    chocolate, chopped
2 tbsp brandy (optional)

For the roulade:
5 large eggs, separated

3 tbsp cocoa powder, sifted,
    plus extra for dusting
125 g/4 oz icing sugar, sifted,
    plus extra for dusting
¼ tsp cream of tartar

For the filling:
175 g/6 oz cranberry sauce

1–2 tbsp brandy (optional)
450 ml/¾ pint double cream,
    whipped to soft peaks

To decorate:
caramelised orange strips
dried cranberries

Preheat the oven to 200°C /400°F/Gas Mark 6. Bring the cream to the boil over a medium heat. Remove from the heat and add all of the chocolate, stirring until melted. Stir in the brandy, if using and strain into a medium bowl. Cool, then refrigerate for 6–8 hours.

Line a 39 x 26 cm/15½ x 10½ inch Swiss roll tin with non-stick baking paper. Using an electric whisk, beat the egg yolks until thick and creamy. Slowly beat in the cocoa powder and half the icing sugar and reserve. Whisk the egg whites and cream of tartar into soft peaks. Gradually whisk in the remaining sugar until the mixture is stiff and glossy. Gently fold the yolk mixture into the egg whites with a metal spoon. Spread evenly into the tin. Bake in the preheated oven for 15 minutes. Remove and invert on to a large sheet of greaseproof paper, dusted with cocoa powder. Cut off the crisp edges of the cake then roll up. Leave on a wire rack until cold.

For the filling, heat the cranberry sauce with the brandy, if using, until warm and spreadable. Unroll the cooled cake and spread with the cranberry sauce. Allow to cool and set. Carefully spoon the whipped cream over the surface and spread to within 2.5 cm/1 inch of the edges. Re-roll the cake. Transfer to a cake plate or tray. Allow the chocolate ganache to soften at room temperature, then beat until soft and of a spreadable consistency. Spread over the roulade and dust with icing sugar. Decorate with the orange strips and cranberries and serve.

Try this: FOR AN ALTERNATIVE: 294   FOR A COOKIE OR TRAYBAKE: 64

Supreme Chocolate Gateau

CUTS INTO 10-12 SLICES

For the cake:
175 g/6 oz self-raising
   flour, sifted
1½ tsp baking powder, sifted
3 tbsp cocoa powder, sifted
175 g/6 oz margarine or

butter, softened
175 g/6 oz caster sugar
3 large eggs

To decorate:
350 g/12 oz plain

dark chocolate
1 gelatine leaf
200 ml/7 fl oz double cream
75 g/3 oz butter
cocoa powder for dusting

Preheat the oven to 180°C/350°F/Gas Mark 4, 10 minutes before baking. Line three 20.5 cm/8 inch round cake tins. Put all the cake ingredients in a bowl and whisk together until thick. Divide the mixture evenly between the prepared tins. Bake in the preheated oven for 35–40 minutes until a skewer inserted in the centre comes out clean. Cool on wire racks.

Very gently heat 2 tablespoons of hot water with 50 g/2 oz of the chocolate and stir until combined. Remove from the heat and leave for 5 minutes. Put the gelatine in a shallow dish and add 2 tablespoons of cold water. Leave for 5 minutes then squeeze out any excess water and add to the chocolate and water mixture. Stir until dissolved. Whip the double cream until just thickened. Add the chocolate mixture and continue whisking until soft peaks form. Leave until starting to set. Place one of the cakes onto a serving plate and spread with half the cream mixture. Top with a second cake and the remaining cream, cover with the third cake and chill in the refrigerator until the cream has set.

Melt 175 g/6 oz of the chocolate with the butter, stir until smooth and leave until thickened. Melt the remaining chocolate. Cut twelve 10 cm/4 inch squares of tinfoil. Spread the chocolate evenly over the squares to within 2.5 cm/1 inch of the edges. Refrigerate for 3–4 minutes until just set but not brittle. Gather up the corners and crimp together. Return to the refrigerator until firm. Spread the chocolate and butter mixture over the top and sides of the cake. Remove the foil from the curls and use to decorate. Dust with cocoa powder and serve.

Try this: FOR AN ALTERNATIVE: 300   FOR A COOKIE OR TRAYBAKE: 130

Black Forest Gateau

CUTS 10-12 SLICES

250 g/9 oz butter
1 tbsp instant coffee
   granules
350 ml/12 fl oz hot water
200 g/7 oz plain dark
   chocolate, chopped

or broken
400 g/14 oz caster sugar
225 g/8 oz self-raising flour
150 g/5 oz plain flour
50 g/2 oz cocoa powder
2 medium eggs

2 tsp vanilla essence
2 x 400 g cans stoned
   cherries in juice
2 tsp arrowroot
600 ml/1 pint double cream
50 ml/2 fl oz kirsch

Preheat the oven to 150˚C/300˚F/Gas Mark 2, 5 minutes before baking. Lightly oil and line a
deep 23 cm/9 inch cake tin. Melt the butter in a large saucepan. Blend the coffee with the hot
water, add to the butter with the chocolate and sugar and heat gently, stirring until smooth.
Pour into a large bowl and leave until just warm.

Sift together the flours and cocoa powder. Using an electric mixer, whisk the warm chocolate
mixture on a low speed, then gradually whisk in the dry ingredients. Whisk in the eggs one at a
time, then the vanilla essence. Pour the mixture into the prepared tin and bake in the
preheated oven for 1 hour 45 minutes or until firm and a skewer inserted into the centre
comes out clean. Leave in the tin for 5 minutes to cool slightly before turning out onto a wire
rack. Place the cherries and their juice in a small saucepan and heat gently. Blend the
arrowroot with 2 teaspoons of water until smooth, then stir into the cherries. Cook, stirring,
until the liquid thickens. Simmer very gently for 2 minutes, then leave until cold.

Whisk the double cream until thick. Trim the top of the cake if necessary, then split the cake
into three layers. Brush the base of the cake with half the kirsch. Top with a layer of cream
and one third of the cherries. Repeat the layering, then place the third layer on top. Reserve
a little cream for decorating and use the remainder to cover the top and sides of the cake.
Pipe a decorative edge around the cake, then arrange the remaining cherries in the centre
and serve.

Try this: FOR AN ALTERNATIVE: 298   FOR A COOKIE OR TRAYBAKE: 84

Cheesecakes & Cake Puddings

Ricotta Cheesecake with Strawberry Coulis

SERVES 6–8

125 g/4 oz digestive biscuits
100 g/3½ oz candied peel, chopped
65 g/2½ oz butter, melted
150 ml/¼ pint crème fraîche

575 g/4 oz ricotta cheese
100 g/3½ oz caster sugar
1 vanilla pod, seeds only
2 large eggs
225 g/8 oz strawberries

25–50 g/1–2 oz caster sugar, to taste
zest and juice of 1 orange

Preheat oven to 170˚C/325˚F/Gas Mark 3. Line a 20.5 cm/8 inch springform tin with baking parchment. Place the biscuits into a food processor together with the peel. Blend until the biscuits are crushed and the peel is chopped. Add 50 g/2 oz of the melted butter and process until mixed. Tip into the tin and spread evenly over the bottom. Press firmly into place and reserve.

Blend together the crème fraîche, ricotta cheese, sugar, vanilla seeds and eggs in a food processor. With the motor running, add the remaining melted butter and blend for a few seconds. Pour the mixture on to the base. Transfer to the preheated oven and cook for about 1 hour, until set and risen round the edges, but slightly wobbly in the centre. Switch off the oven and allow to cool there. chill in the refrigerator for at least 8 hours, or preferably overnight.

Wash and drain the strawberries. Hull the fruit and remove any soft spots. Put into the food processor along with 25 g/1 oz of the sugar and orange juice and zest. Blend until smooth. Add the remaining sugar to taste. Pass through a sieve to remove seeds and chill in the refrigerator until needed.

Cut the cheesecake into wedges, spoon over some of the strawberry coulis and serve.

Try this: FOR AN ALTERNATIVE: 316 FOR A CAKE: 232

Baked Lemon &
Sultana Cheesecake

CUTS INTO 10 SLICES

275 g/10 oz caster sugar
50 g/2 oz butter
50 g/2 oz self-raising flour
½ level tsp baking powder
5 large eggs
450 g/1 lb cream cheese

40 g/1½ oz plain flour
grated rind of 1 lemon
3 tbsp fresh lemon juice
150 ml/¼ pint crème fraîche
75 g/3 oz sultanas

To decorate:
1 tbsp icing sugar
fresh blackcurrants or
    blueberries
mint leaves

Preheat the oven to 170°C/325°F/Gas Mark 3. Oil a 20.5 cm/8 inch loose-bottomed round cake tin with non-stick baking paper.

Beat 50 g/2 oz of the sugar and the butter together until light and creamy, then stir in the self-raising flour, baking powder and 1 egg. Mix lightly together until well blended. Spoon into the prepared tin and spread the mixture over the base. Separate the four remaining eggs and reserve.

Blend the cheese in a food processor until soft. Gradually add the eggs yolks and sugar and blend until smooth. Turn into a bowl and stir in the rest of the flour, lemon rind and juice. Mix lightly before adding the crème fraîche and sultanas, stirring well.

Whisk the egg whites until stiff, fold into the cheese mixture and pour into the tin. Tap lightly on the surface to remove any air bubbles. Bake in the preheated oven for about 1 hour, or until golden and firm. Cover lightly if browning too much. Switch the oven off and leave in the oven to cool for 2–3 hours.

Remove the cheesecake from the oven and, when completely cold, remove from the tin. Sprinkle with the icing sugar, decorate with the blackcurrants or blueberries and mint leaves and serve.

Try this: FOR AN ALTERNATIVE: 2310   FOR A CAKE: 188

Chocolate & Saffron Cheesecake

SERVES 6

¼ tsp saffron threads
175 g/6 oz plain flour
pinch of salt
75 g/3 oz butter
1 tbsp caster sugar
1 medium egg yolk

350 g/12 oz curd cheese
75 g/3 oz golden
   granulated sugar
125 g/4 oz plain dark
   chocolate, melted
   and cooled

6 tbsp milk
3 medium eggs
1 tbsp icing sugar,
   sifted, to decorate

Preheat the oven to 200°C/400°F/Gas Mark 6, 15 minutes before baking. Lightly oil a
20.5 cm/8 inch fluted flan tin. Soak the saffron threads in 1 tablespoon of hot water for
20 minutes. Sift the flour and salt into a bowl. Cut the butter into small cubes, then add to the
flour and using your fingertips, rub in the butter until the mixture resembles breadcrumbs. Stir
in the sugar. Beat the egg yolk with 1 tablespoon of cold water, add to the mixture and mix
together until a smooth and pliable dough is formed. Add a little extra water if necessary.
Knead on a lightly floured surface until free from cracks, then wrap in clingfilm and chill in the
refrigerator for 30 minutes. Roll the pastry out on a lightly floured surface and use to line the
flan tin. Prick the pastry base and sides with a fork and line with non-stick baking parchment
and baking beans. Bake blind in the preheated oven for 12 minutes. Remove the beans and
baking parchment and continue to bake blind for 5 minutes.

Beat together the curd cheese and granulated sugar, then beat in the melted chocolate,
saffron liquid, the milk and eggs, mix until blended thoroughly. Pour the mixture into the
cooked flan case and place on a baking sheet. Reduce the oven temperature to
190°C/375°F/Gas Mark 5 and bake for 15 minutes, then reduce the oven temperature to
180°C/350°F/Gas Mark 4 and continue to bake for 20–30 minutes or until set. Remove the
cheesecake from the oven and leave for 10 minutes before removing from the flan tin, if
serving warm. If serving cold, leave in the flan tin to cool before removing and placing on a
serving platter. Sprinkle with icing sugar before serving.

Try this: FOR AN ALTERNATIVE: 312   FOR A CAKE: 284

Orange Chocolate Cheesecake

SERVES 8

225 g/8 oz plain chocolate
coated digestive biscuits
50 g/2 oz butter
450 g/1 lb mixed fruits, such
as blueberries and
raspberries

1 tbsp icing sugar, sifted
few sprigs of fresh mint,
to decorate

For the filling:
450 g/1 lb soft cream cheese

1 tbsp gelatine
350 g/12 oz orange
chocolate, broken
into segments
600 ml/1 pint double cream

Lightly oil and line a 20.5 cm/8 inch round loose-based cake tin with non-stick baking parchment. Place the biscuits in a polythene bag and crush using a rolling pin. Alternatively, use a food processor. Melt the butter in a medium-sized, heavy-based saucepan, add the crushed biscuits and mix well. Press the biscuit mixture into the base of the lined tin, then chill in the refrigerator for 20 minutes.

For the filling, remove the cream cheese from the refrigerator, at least 20 minutes before using, to allow the cheese to come to room temperature. Place the cream cheese in a bowl and beat until smooth, reserve. Pour 4 tablespoons of water into a small bowl and sprinkle over the gelatine. Leave to stand for 5 minutes until spongy. Place the bowl over a saucepan of simmering water and allow to dissolve, stirring occasionally. Leave to cool slightly.

Melt the orange chocolate in a heatproof bowl set over a saucepan of simmering water, then leave to cool slightly. Whip the cream until soft peaks form. Beat the gelatine and chocolate into cream cheese. Fold in the cream. Spoon into the tin and level the surface. Chill in the refrigerator for 4 hours until set.

Remove the cheesecake from the tin and place on a serving plate. Top with the fruits, dust with icing sugar and decorate with sprigs of mint.

Try this: FOR AN ALTERNATIVE: 306   FOR A CAKE: 260

White Chocolate Cheesecake

CUTS INTO 16 SLICES

For the base:
150 g/5 oz digestive biscuits
50 g/2 oz whole almonds,
    lightly toasted
50 g/2 oz butter, melted
½ tsp almond essence

For the filling:
350 g/12 oz good-quality
    white chocolate, chopped
125 ml/4 fl oz double cream
700 g/1½ lb cream
    cheese, softened
50 g/2 oz caster sugar
4 large eggs

2 tbsp Amaretto or
    almond-flavour liqueur
For the topping:
450 ml/¾ pint soured cream
50 g/2 oz caster sugar
½ tsp almond or vanilla essence
white chocolate curls,
    to decorate

Preheat the oven to 180°C/350°F/Gas Mark 4, 10 minutes before baking. Lightly oil a 23 x 7.5 cm/9 x 3 inch springform tin. Crush the biscuits and almonds in a food processor to form fine crumbs. Pour in the butter and almond essence and blend. Pour the crumbs into the tin and using the back of a spoon, press on to the bottom and up the sides to within 1 cm/½ inch of the top of the tin. Bake in the preheated oven for 5 minutes to set. Remove and transfer to a wire rack. Reduce the oven temperature to 150°C/300°F/Gas Mark 2.

Heat the white chocolate and cream in a saucepan over a low heat, stirring until melted, then cool. Beat the cream cheese and sugar until smooth. Add the eggs, one at a time, beating well after each. Slowly beat in the cooled white chocolate cream and the Amaretto and pour into the baked crust. Place on a baking tray and bake for 45–55 minutes, until the edge of the cake is firm, but the centre is slightly soft. Reduce the oven temperature if the top begins to brown. Remove to a wire rack and increase the temperature to 200°C/400°F/Gas Mark 6.

To make the topping, beat the soured cream, sugar and almond or vanilla essence until smooth and pour evenly over the cheesecake. Bake for another 5 minutes to set. Turn off the oven and leave the door halfway open for about 1 hour. Transfer to a wire rack and run a sharp knife around the edge to separate from the tin. Refrigerate until chilled. Remove from the tin, decorate with white chocolate curls and serve.

Try this: FOR AN ALTERNATIVE: 314 FOR A CAKE: 246

Triple Chocolate Cheesecake

SERVES 6

For the base:
150 g/5 oz digestive
biscuits, crushed
50 g/2 oz butter, melted

For the cheesecake:
75 g/3 oz white chocolate,

roughly chopped
300 ml/½ pint double cream
50 g/2 oz caster sugar
3 medium eggs, beaten
400 g/14 oz full fat soft
cream cheese
2 tbsp cornflour

75 g/3 oz plain dark
chocolate, roughly
chopped
75 g/3 oz milk chocolate,
roughly chopped
fromage frais,
to serve

Preheat the oven to 180°C/350°F/Gas Mark 4, 10 minutes before baking. Lightly oil a 23 x 7.5 cm/9 x 3 inch springform tin.

To make the base, mix together the crushed biscuits and melted butter. Press into the base of the tin and leave to set. Chill in the refrigerator.

Place the white chocolate and cream in a small, heavy-based saucepan and heat gently until the chocolate has melted. Stir until smooth and reserve. Beat the sugar and eggs together until light and creamy in colour, add the cream cheese and beat until the mixture is smooth and free from lumps. Stir the reserved white chocolate cream together with the cornflour into the soft cream cheese mixture.

Add the dark and milk chocolate to the soft cream cheese mixture and mix lightly together until blended. Spoon over the chilled base, place on a baking sheet and bake in the preheated oven for 1 hour.

Switch off the heat, open the oven door and leave the cheesecake to cool in the oven. Chill in the refrigerator for at least 6 hours before removing the cheesecake from the tin. Cut into slices and transfer to serving plates. Serve with fromage frais.

Try this: FOR AN ALTERNATIVE: 308 FOR A CAKE: 280

Summer Fruit Semifreddo

SERVES 6–8

225 g/8 oz raspberries
125 g/4 oz blueberries
125 g/4 oz redcurrants
50 g/2 oz icing sugar

juice of 1 lemon
1 vanilla pod, split
50 g/2 oz sugar
4 large eggs, separated

600 ml/1 pint double cream
pinch of salt
fresh redcurrants,
    to decorate

Wash and hull or remove stalks from the fruits, as necessary, then put them into a food processor or blender with the icing sugar and lemon juice. Blend to a purée, pour into a jug and chill in the refrigerator, until needed.

Remove the seeds from the vanilla pod by opening the pod and scraping with the back of a knife. Add the seeds to the sugar and whisk with the egg yolks until pale and thick.

In another bowl, whip the cream until soft peaks form. Do not overwhip. In a third bowl, whip the egg whites with the salt until stiff peaks form.

Using a large metal spoon – to avoid knocking any air from the mixture – fold together the fruit purée, egg yolk mixture, the cream and egg whites. Transfer the mixture to a round, shallow, lidded freezer box and put into the freezer until almost frozen. If the mixture freezes solid, thaw in the refrigerator until semi-frozen. Turn out the semi-frozen mixture, cut into wedges and serve decorated with a few fresh redcurrants. If the mixture thaws completely, eat immediately and do not refreeze.

Try this: FOR AN ALTERNATIVE: 304 FOR A CAKE: 240

Eve's Pudding

SERVES 6

450 g/1 lb cooking apples	125 g/4 oz caster sugar	125 g/4 oz self-raising flour
175 g/6 oz blackberries	125 g/4 oz butter	1 tbsp icing sugar
75 g/3 oz demerara sugar	few drops of vanilla essence	ready-made custard,
grated rind of 1 lemon	2 medium eggs, beaten	to serve

Preheat the oven to 180°C/350°F/Gas Mark 4. Oil a 1.1 litre/2 pint baking dish.

Peel, core and slice the apples and place a layer in the base of the prepared dish. Sprinkle over some of the blackberries, a little demerara sugar and lemon zest. Continue to layer the apple and blackberries in this way until all the ingredients have been used.

Cream the sugar and butter together until light and fluffy. Beat in the vanilla essence and then the eggs a little at a time, adding a spoonful of flour after each addition. Fold in the extra flour with a metal spoon or rubber spatula and mix well. Spread the sponge mixture over the top of the fruit and level with the back of a spoon.

Place the dish on a baking sheet and bake in the preheated oven for 35–40 minutes, or until well risen and golden brown. To test if the pudding is cooked, press the cooked sponge lightly with a clean finger – if it springs back the sponge is cooked.

Dust the pudding with a little icing sugar and serve immediately with the custard.

Try this: FOR AN ALTERNATIVE: 324   FOR A CAKE: 228

Lemon & Apricot Pudding

SERVES 4

125 g/4 oz ready-to-eat
   dried apricots
3 tbsp orange juice, warmed
50 g/2 oz butter

125 g/4 oz caster sugar
juice and grated rind of
   2 lemons
2 medium eggs

50 g/2 oz self-raising flour
300 ml/½ pint milk
custard or fresh cream,
   to serve

Preheat the oven to 180°C/350°F/Gas Mark 4. Oil a 1.1 litre/2 pint pie dish.

Soak the apricots in the orange juice for 10–15 minutes or until most of the juice has been absorbed, then place in the base of the pie dish.

Cream the butter and sugar together with the lemon rind until light and fluffy. Separate the eggs. Beat the egg yolks into the creamed mixture with a spoonful of flour after each addition. Add the remaining flour and beat well until smooth.

Stir the milk and lemon juice into the creamed mixture. Whisk the egg whites in a grease-free mixing bowl until stiff and standing in peaks. Fold into the mixture using a metal spoon or rubber spatula.

Pour into the prepared dish and place in a baking tray filled with enough cold water to come halfway up the sides of the dish.

Bake in the preheated oven for about 45 minutes, or until the sponge is firm and golden brown. Remove from the oven. Serve immediately with the custard or fresh cream.

Try this: FOR AN ALTERNATIVE: 322   FOR A CAKE: 224

Lemon Surprise

SERVES 4

75 g/3 oz margarine
175 g/6 oz caster sugar
3 medium eggs, separated
75 g/3 oz self-raising flour

450 ml/¾ pint semi-
    skimmed milk
juice of 2 lemons
juice of 1 orange

2 tsp icing sugar
lemon twists, to decorate
sliced strawberries,
    to serve

Preheat the oven to 190°C/375°F/Gas Mark 5. Lightly oil a deep ovenproof dish.

Beat together the margarine and sugar until pale and fluffy. Add the egg yolks, one at a time, with 1 tablespoon of the flour and beat well after each addition. Once added, stir in the remaining flour. Stir in the milk, 4 tablespoons of the lemon juice and 3 tablespoons of the orange juice.

Whisk the egg whites until stiff and fold into the pudding mixture with a metal spoon or rubber spatula until well combined. Pour into the prepared dish.

Stand the dish in a roasting tin and pour in just enough boiling water to come halfway up the sides of the dish. Bake in the preheated oven for 45 minutes, until well risen and spongy to the touch.

Remove the pudding from the oven and sprinkle with the icing sugar. Decorate with the lemon twists and serve immediately with the strawberries.

Try this: FOR AN ALTERNATIVE: 320   FOR A CAKE: 252

Golden Castle Pudding

SERVES 4-6

125 g/4 oz butter
125 g/4 oz caster sugar
a few drops of

vanilla essence
2 medium eggs, beaten
125 g/4 oz self-raising flour

4 tbsp golden syrup
crème fraîche or ready-made
custard, to serve

Preheat the oven to 180˚C/350˚F/Gas Mark 4. Lightly oil four to six individual pudding bowls and place a small circle of lightly oiled non-stick greaseproof paper in the base of each one.

Place the butter and caster sugar in a large bowl, then beat together until the mixture is pale and creamy. Stir in the vanilla essence and gradually add the beaten eggs, a little at a time. Add a tablespoon of flour after each addition of egg and beat well.

When the mixture is smooth, add the remaining flour and fold in gently. Add a tablespoon of water and mix to form a soft mixture that will drop easily off a spoon.

Spoon enough mixture into each basin to come halfway up the tin, allowing enough space for the puddings to rise. Place on a baking sheet and bake in the preheated oven for about 25 minutes until firm and golden brown.

Allow the puddings to stand for 5 minutes. Discard the paper circles and turn out on to individual serving plates.

Warm the golden syrup in a small saucepan and pour a little over each pudding. Serve hot with the crème fraîche or custard.

Try this: FOR AN ALTERNATIVE: 318 FOR A CAKE: 208

Cherry Batter Pudding

SERVES 4

450 g/1 lb fresh cherries (or
425 g can pitted cherries)
50 g/2 oz plain flour
pinch of salt

3 tbsp caster sugar
2 medium eggs
300 ml/1½ pint milk
40 g/1½ oz butter

1 tbsp rum
extra caster sugar, to dredge
fresh cream, to serve

Preheat the oven to 220°C/425°F/Gas Mark 7. Lightly oil a 900 ml/1½ pint shallow
baking dish.

Rinse the cherries, drain well and remove the stones (using a cherry stoner if possible). If
using canned cherries, drain well, discard the juice and place in the prepared dish.

Sift the flour and salt into a large bowl. Stir in 2 tablespoons of the caster sugar and make a
well in the centre. Beat the eggs, then pour into the well of the dry ingredients. Warm the milk
and slowly pour into the well, beating throughout and gradually drawing in the flour from the
sides of the bowl. Continue until a smooth batter has formed.

Melt the butter in a small saucepan over a low heat, then stir into the batter with the rum.
Reserve for 15 minutes, then beat again until smooth and easy to pour. Pour into the prepared
baking dish and bake in the preheated oven for 30–35 minutes, or until golden brown and set.

Remove the pudding from the oven, sprinkle with the remaining sugar and serve hot with
plenty of fresh cream.

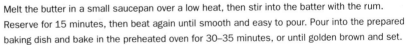

Try this: FOR AN ALTERNATIVE: 328 FOR A CAKE: 256

Jam Roly Poly

SERVES 6

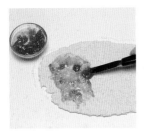

225 g/8 oz self-raising flour
¼ tsp salt
125 g/4 oz shredded suet

about 150 ml/¼ pint water
3 tbsp strawberry jam
1 tbsp milk, to glaze

1 tsp caster sugar
ready-made jam sauce,
to serve

Preheat the oven to 200°C/400°F/Gas Mark 6.

Make the pastry by sifting the flour and salt into a large bowl. Add the suet and mix lightly,
then add the water a little at a time and mix to form a soft and pliable dough – take care not to
make the dough too wet.

Turn the dough out on to a lightly floured board and knead gently until smooth. Roll the dough
out into a 23 x 28 cm/9 x 11 inch rectangle. Spread the jam over the pastry leaving a border
of 1 cm/½ inch all round. Fold the border over the jam and brush the edges with water.

Lightly roll the rectangle up from one of the short sides, seal the top edge and press the ends
together. Do not roll the pudding up too tightly. Turn the pudding upside down on to a large
piece of greaseproof paper large enough to come halfway up the sides.

Tie the ends of the paper, to make a boat-shaped paper case for the pudding to sit in and to
leave plenty of room for the roly poly to expand.

Brush the pudding lightly with milk and sprinkle with the sugar. Bake in the preheated oven for
30–40 minutes, or until well risen and golden. Serve immediately with the jam sauce.

Try this: FOR AN ALTERNATIVE: 326   FOR A CAKE: 234

College Pudding

SERVES 4

125 g/4 oz shredded suet
125 g/4 oz fresh
   white breadcrumbs
50 g/2 oz sultanas

50 g/2 oz seedless raisins
½ tsp ground cinnamon
¼ tsp freshly grated nutmeg
¼ tsp mixed spice

50 g/2 oz caster sugar
½ tsp baking powder
2 medium eggs, beaten
orange zest, to garnish

Preheat the oven to 180°C/350°F/Gas Mark 4. Lightly oil an ovenproof 900 ml/1½ pint ovenproof pudding basin and place a small circle of greaseproof paper in the base.

Mix the shredded suet and breadcrumbs together and rub lightly together with the fingertips to remove any lumps.

Stir in the dried fruit, spices, sugar and baking powder. Add the eggs and beat lightly together until the mixture is well blended and the fruit is evenly distributed.

Spoon the mixture into the prepared pudding basin and level the surface. Place on a baking tray and cover lightly with some greaseproof paper.

Bake in the preheated oven for 20 minutes, then remove the paper and continue to bake for a further 10–15 minutes, or until the top is firm.

When the pudding is cooked, remove from the oven and carefully turn out on to a warmed serving dish. Decorate with the orange zest and serve immediately.

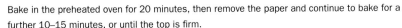

Try this: FOR AN ALTERNATIVE: 334 FOR A CAKE: 182

Topsy Turvy Pudding

SERVES 6

For the topping:
175 g/6 oz demerara sugar
2 oranges

For the sponge:
175 g/6 oz butter, softened

175 g/6 oz caster sugar
3 medium eggs, beaten
175 g/6 oz self-raising
   flour, sifted
50 g/2 oz plain dark
   chocolate, melted

grated rind of 1 orange
25 g/1 oz cocoa
   powder, sifted
custard or soured cream,
   to serve

Preheat the oven to 180°C/350°F/Gas Mark 4, 10 minutes before baking. Lightly oil a 20.5 cm/8 inch deep round loose-based cake tin. Place the demerara sugar and 3 tablespoons of water in a small, heavy-based saucepan and heat gently until the sugar has dissolved. Swirl the saucepan or stir with a clean wooden spoon to ensure the sugar has dissolved, then bring to the boil and boil rapidly until a golden caramel is formed. Pour into the base of the tin and leave to cool.

For the sponge, cream the butter and sugar together until light and fluffy. Gradually beat in the eggs a little at a time, beating well between each addition. Add a spoonful of flour after each addition to prevent the mixture curdling. Add the melted chocolate and then stir well. Fold in the orange rind, self-raising flour and sifted cocoa powder and mix well.

Remove the peel from both oranges taking care to remove as much of the pith as possible. Thinly slice the peel into strips and then slice the oranges. Arrange the peel and then the orange slices over the caramel. Top with the sponge mixture and level the top.

Place the tin on a baking sheet and bake in the preheated oven for 40–45 minutes or until well risen, golden brown and an inserted skewer comes out clean. Remove from the oven, leave for about 5 minutes, invert onto a serving plate and sprinkle with cocoa powder. Serve with either custard or soured cream.

Try this: FOR AN ALTERNATIVE: 340 FOR A CAKE: 260

Nutty Date Pudding with Chocolate Sauce

SERVES 6-8

125 g/4 oz butter, softened
125 g/4 oz golden caster sugar
3 medium eggs, beaten
175 g/6 oz self-raising flour, sifted
50 g/2 oz plain dark chocolate, grated

3 tbsp milk
75 g/3 oz hazelnuts, roughly chopped
75 g/3 oz stoned dates, roughly chopped
chopped toasted hazelnuts, to serve

For the chocolate sauce:
50 g/2 oz unsalted butter
50 g/2 oz soft light brown sugar
50 g/2 oz plain dark chocolate, broken into pieces
125 ml/4 fl oz double cream

Lightly oil a 1.1 litre/2 pint pudding basin and line the base with a small circle of non-stick baking parchment. Cream the butter and sugar together in a large bowl until light and fluffy. Add the beaten eggs a little at a time, adding 1 tablespoon of the flour after each addition. When all the eggs have been added, stir in the remaining flour. Add the grated chocolate and mix in lightly, then stir in the milk together with the hazelnuts and dates. Stir lightly until mixed well. Spoon the mixture into the pudding basin and level the surface. Cover with a double sheet of baking parchment with a pleat in the centre, allowing for expansion, then cover either with a pudding cloth or a double sheet of tinfoil, again with a central pleat. Secure with string.

Place in the top of a steamer, set over a saucepan of gently simmering water and steam for 2 hours, or until cooked and firm to the touch. Remember to top up the water if necessary. Remove the pudding from the saucepan and leave to rest for 5 minutes, before turning out onto a serving plate. Discard the small circle of baking parchment, then sprinkle with the chopped toasted hazelnuts. Keep warm.

Meanwhile, make the sauce. Place the butter, sugar and chocolate in a saucepan and heat until the chocolate has melted. Stir in the cream and simmer for 3 minutes until thickened. Pour over the pudding and serve.

Try this: FOR AN ALTERNATIVE: 344 FOR A CAKE: 264

Chocolate Sponge Pudding
with Fudge Sauce

SERVES 4

75 g/3 oz butter
75 g/3 oz caster sugar
50 g/2 oz plain dark
   chocolate, melted
50 g/2 oz self-raising flour
25 g/1 oz drinking chocolate

1 large egg
1 tbsp icing sugar, to dust
crème fraîche, to serve

For the fudge sauce:
50 g/2 oz soft light brown sugar

1 tbsp cocoa powder
40 g/1½ oz pecan nuts,
   roughly chopped
25 g/1 oz caster sugar
300 ml/½ pint hot, strong
   black coffee

Preheat the oven to 170°C/ 325°F/Gas Mark 3. Oil a 900 ml/1½ pint pie dish.

Cream the butter and the sugar together in a large bowl until light and fluffy. Stir in the melted chocolate, flour, drinking chocolate and egg and mix together. Turn the mixture into the prepared dish and level the surface.

To make the fudge sauce, blend the brown sugar, cocoa powder and pecan nuts together and sprinkle evenly over the top of the pudding.

Stir the caster sugar into the hot black coffee until it has dissolved. Carefully pour the coffee over the top of the pudding.

Bake in the preheated oven for 50–60 minutes, until the top is firm to touch. There will now be a rich sauce underneath the sponge. Remove from the oven, dust with icing sugar and serve hot with crème fraîche.

Try this: FOR AN ALTERNATIVE: 338   FOR A CAKE: 274

Individual Steamed Chocolate Puddings

SERVES 8

150 g/5 oz unsalted
  butter, softened
175 g/6 oz light
  muscovado sugar
½ tsp freshly grated nutmeg

25 g/1 oz plain white flour, sifted
4 tbsp cocoa powder, sifted
5 medium eggs, separated
125 g/4 oz ground almonds
50 g/2 oz white breadcrumbs

To serve:
Greek yogurt
orange-flavoured
  chocolate curls

Preheat the oven to 180°C/350°F/Gas Mark 4, 10 minutes before baking. Lightly oil and line the bases of eight individual 175 ml/6 fl oz pudding basins with a small circle of non-stick baking parchment.

Cream the butter with 50 g/2 oz of the sugar and the nutmeg until light and fluffy. Sift the flour and cocoa powder together, then stir into the creamed mixture. Beat in the egg yolks and mix well, then fold in the ground almonds and the breadcrumbs.

Whisk the egg whites in a clean, grease-free bowl until stiff and standing in peaks then gradually whisk in the remaining sugar. Using a metal spoon, fold a quarter of the egg whites into the chocolate mixture and mix well, then fold in the remaining egg whites.

Spoon the mixture into the prepared basins, filling them two thirds full to allow for expansion. Cover with a double sheet of tinfoil and secure tightly with string. Stand the pudding basins in a roasting tin and pour in sufficient water to come halfway up the sides of the basins.

Bake in the centre of the preheated oven for 30 minutes, or until the puddings are firm to the touch. Remove from the oven, loosen around the edges and invert onto warmed serving plates. Serve immediately with Greek yogurt and chocolate curls.

Try this: FOR AN ALTERNATIVE: 348   FOR A CAKE: 278

Chocolate Pear Pudding

SERVES 6

140 g/4½ oz butter, softened
2 tbsp soft brown sugar
400 g can of pear halves,
    drained and juice
    reserved

25 g/1 oz walnut halves
125 g/4 oz golden caster
    sugar
2 medium eggs, beaten
75 g/3 oz self-raising

flour, sifted
50 g/2 oz cocoa powder
1 tsp baking powder
prepared chocolate custard,
    to serve

Preheat the oven to 190°C/375°F/Gas Mark 5, 10 minutes before baking. Butter a 20.5 cm/
8 inch sandwich tin with 15 g/½ oz of the butter and sprinkle the base with the soft brown
sugar. Arrange the drained pear halves on top of the sugar, cut-side down. Fill the spaces
between the pears with the walnut halves, flat-side upwards.

Cream the remaining butter with the caster sugar then gradually beat in the beaten eggs,
adding 1 tablespoon of the flour after each addition. When all the eggs have been added, stir
in the remaining flour.

Sift the cocoa powder and baking powder together, then stir into the creamed mixture with
1–2 tablespoons of the reserved pear juice to give a smooth dropping consistency.

Spoon the mixture over the pear halves, smoothing the surface. Bake in the preheated oven
for 20–25 minutes, or until well risen and the surface springs back when lightly pressed.

Remove from the oven and leave to cool for 5 minutes. Using a palate knife, loosen the sides
and invert onto a serving plate. Serve with custard.

Try this: FOR AN ALTERNATIVE: 342 FOR A CAKE: 216

Peach & Chocolate Bake

SERVES 6

200 g/7 oz plain dark
   chocolate
125 g/4 oz unsalted butter
4 medium eggs, separated

125 g/4 oz caster sugar
425 g can peach slices,
   drained
½ tsp ground cinnamon

1 tbsp icing sugar, sifted,
   to decorate
crème fraîche, to serve

Preheat the oven to 170˚C/325˚F/Gas Mark 3, 10 minutes before baking. Lightly oil a
1.7 litre/3 pint ovenproof dish.

Break the chocolate and butter into small pieces and place in a small heatproof bowl set over
a saucepan of gently simmering water. Ensure the water is not touching the base of the bowl
and leave to melt. Remove the bowl from the heat and stir until smooth.

Whisk the egg yolks with the sugar until very thick and creamy, then stir the melted chocolate
and butter into the whisked egg yolk mixture and mix together lightly.

Place the egg whites in a clean, grease-free bowl and whisk until stiff, then fold 2 tablespoons
of the whisked egg whites into the chocolate mixture. Mix well, then add the remaining egg
white and fold in very lightly.

Fold the peach slices and the cinnamon into the mixture, then spoon the mixture into the
prepared dish. Do not level the mixture – leave the surface a little uneven.

Bake in the preheated oven for 35–40 minutes, or until well risen and just firm to the touch.
Sprinkle the bake with the icing sugar and serve immediately with spoonfuls of crème fraîche.

Try this: FOR AN ALTERNATIVE: 340   FOR A CAKE: 244

Fruity Chocolate Puddings with Sticky Chocolate Sauce

SERVES 4

125 g/4 oz dark
  muscovado sugar
1 orange, peeled and
  segmented
75 g/3 oz cranberries, fresh
  or thawed if frozen
125g/4 oz soft margarine

2 medium eggs
75 g/3 oz plain flour
½ tsp baking powder
3 tbsp cocoa powder
chocolate curls,
  to decorate

For the sticky chocolate sauce:
175 g/6 oz plain dark
  chocolate, broken into pieces
50 g/2 oz butter
50 g/2 oz caster sugar
2 tbsp golden syrup
200 ml/7 fl oz milk

Lightly oil four 200 ml/7 fl oz individual pudding basins and sprinkle with a little of the muscovado sugar. Place a few orange segments in each basin followed by a spoonful of the cranberries. Cream the remaining muscovado sugar with the margarine until light and fluffy, then gradually beat in the eggs a little at a time, adding 1 tablespoon of the flour after each addition. Sift the remaining flour, baking powder and cocoa powder together, then stir into the creamed mixture with 1 tablespoon of cooled boiled water to give a soft dropping consistency. Spoon the mixture into the basins.

Cover each pudding with a double sheet of non-stick baking parchment with a pleat in the centre and secure tightly with string. Cover with a double sheet of tinfoil. Place in the top of a steamer, set over a saucepan of gently simmering water and steam steadily for 45 minutes, or until firm to the touch. Remember to replenish the water if necessary. Remove the puddings from the steamer and leave to rest for about 5 minutes before running a knife around the edges of the puddings and turning out onto individual plates.

Meanwhile, make the chocolate sauce. Melt the chocolate and butter in a heatproof bowl set over a saucepan of gently simmering water. Add the sugar and golden syrup and stir until dissolved, then stir in the milk and continue to cook, stirring often, until the sauce thickens. Decorate the puddings with a few chocolate curls and serve with the sauce.

Try this: FOR AN ALTERNATIVE: 332 FOR A CAKE: 296

Sticky Chocolate Surprise Pudding

SERVES 6-8

150 g/5 oz self-raising flour
25 g/1 oz cocoa powder
200 g/7 oz golden
    caster sugar
75 g/3 oz mint-flavoured
    chocolate, chopped

175 ml/6 fl oz full cream milk
2 tsp vanilla essence
50 g/2 oz unsalted butter,
    melted
1 medium egg
sprig of fresh mint, to decorate

For the sauce:
175 g/6 oz dark muscovado
    sugar
125 g/4 oz cocoa powder
600 ml/1 pint very hot water

Preheat the oven to 180°C/350°F/Gas Mark 4, 10 minutes before baking. Lightly oil a
1.4 litre/2½ pint ovenproof soufflé dish. Sift the flour and cocoa powder into a large bowl
and stir in the caster sugar and the chopped mint-flavoured chocolate and make a well in
the centre.

Whisk the milk, vanilla essence and the melted butter together, then beat in the egg. Pour into
the well in the dry ingredients and gradually mix together, drawing the dry ingredients in from
the sides of the bowl. Beat well until mixed thoroughly. Spoon into the prepared soufflé dish.

To make the sauce, blend the dark muscovado sugar and the cocoa powder together and
spoon over the top of the pudding. Carefully pour the hot water over the top of the pudding,
but do not mix.

Bake in the preheated oven for 35–40 minutes, or until firm to the touch and the mixture has
formed a sauce underneath. Decorate with mint and serve immediately.

Try this: FOR AN ALTERNATIVE: 336   FOR A CAKE: 288

Steamed Chocolate Chip Pudding

SERVES 6

175 g/6 oz self-raising flour
½ tsp baking powder
75 g/3 oz fresh white
    breadcrumbs
125 g/4 oz shredded suet
125 g/4 oz golden
    caster sugar

2 medium eggs,
    lightly beaten
1 tsp vanilla essence
125 g/4 oz chocolate chips
150 ml/¼ pint cold milk
grated chocolate,
    to decorate

For the chocolate custard:
300 ml/½ pint milk
1 tbsp cornflour
1 tbsp cocoa powder
1 tbsp caster sugar
½ tsp vanilla essence
1 medium egg yolk

Lightly oil a 1.1 litre/2 pint pudding basin and line the base with a small circle of non-stick baking parchment. Sift the flour and baking powder into a bowl, add the breadcrumbs, suet and sugar and mix well. Stir in the eggs and vanilla essence with the chocolate chips and mix with sufficient cold milk to form a smooth dropping consistency.

Spoon the mixture into the prepared basin and cover the pudding with a double sheet of baking parchment and then either a double sheet of tinfoil or a pudding cloth, with a pleat in the centre to allow for expansion. Secure tightly with string.

Place in the top of a steamer, set over a saucepan of simmering water and steam for 1½–2 hours, or until the pudding is cooked and firm to the touch – replenish the water as necessary. Remove and leave to rest for 5 minutes before turning out onto a warmed serving plate.

Meanwhile, make the custard. Blend a little of the milk with the cornflour and cocoa powder to form a paste. Stir in the remaining milk with the sugar and vanilla essence. Pour into a saucepan and bring to the boil, stirring. Whisk in the egg yolk and cook for 1 minute. Decorate the pudding with grated chocolate and serve with the sauce.

Try this: FOR AN ALTERNATIVE: 338 FOR A CAKE: 294

Index

Index